WE WERE ALWAYS HERE

A Queer Words Anthology

WE WERE ALWAYS HERE

A Queer Words Anthology

Edited by Ryan Vance &
Michael Lee Richardson

Published by 404 Ink
www.404Ink.com
@404Ink

ISBN: 9781912489145
ebook: 9781912489152

Cover design: Ryan Vance
Editors: Ryan Vance & Michael Lee Richardson

Printed and bound in Great Britain
by Clays Ltd, Elcograf S.p.A

The editors acknowledge and are grateful for support from Creative Scotland in the creation & publication of this title.

CREATIVE SCOTLAND
ALBA | CHRUTHACHAIL

LOTTERY FUNDED

CONTENTS

Content Warnings Index.......................................i
Foreword: *Bending Time* by Garry Mac....................ii
Projector by Heather Valentine 1
Queer the Screen II by AR Crow............................11
Katy Perry Remix by AR Crow.............................12
Jellyfish by Jane Flett..13
Adjustment Period by Gray Crosbie........................22
Sequins by Christina Neuwirth..............................23
Cheirotonia at Newhaven by Freddie Alexander........33
301.4157 by Freddie Alexander 35
Borrowed Trouble by Lori England 37
Legacy by Bibi June 45
These Are My Hands by Jo Clifford........................48
Outside, It's Always Summer
by Elaine Gallagher.................................51
Fathers, do not exasperate your children
(Ephesians 6:4) by BD Owens..................57
Tornados Sweep Ballat Cross by BD Owens 59
Circles by Ross Jamieson...61
Excerpt from: *Becoming Doctor Barry*
by MJ Brocklebank................................70
To Be Divine by Callum Harper...........................83
Are You Lonesome Tonight?
by Shane Strachan.................................84
Abolish the Police by Harry Josephine Giles............93
The Middle of Everything by Ciara Maguire............97
Abbie by April Hill 106
Rain by April Hill 108
Harvest by April Hill..110

Stranger Blood is Sweeter by Kirsty Logan 112
Practice by Jack Bigglestone.................................119
Smudged by Sandra Alland 120
deathless by Etzali Hernández...............................126
Ancestry by Etzali Hernández................................128
daughters of god by Etzali Hernández 130
what I see when I see you
by Etzali Hernández 132
Forgive the Rain
by Felicity Anderson-Nathan 134
Recalling by Jay G Ying.......................................140
None of Summer's My Business
by Laura Waddell...................................146
Meules by Eris Young..148
Mary Godwin Shelley's Second Wife
by Alice Tarbuck 157
The Landscaper by Elva Hills 159
Iris, the Oldest Particle Physicist at CERN
by Rachel Plummer.................................169
Titan Arum by Rachel Plummer...........................171
Nimblemen by Rachel Plummer............................172
Selkie by Rachel Plummer 173
Mr. Fox by Heather Parry.....................................174
Dear Christopher by Jonathan Bay........................181
Free Nipple Graft Technique
by Jonathan Bay......................................182
Continental Drift by Zoe Storrie...........................183
IKEA by Andrés Ordorica.......................................192
Not This Again by Jay Whittaker 197
Mausoleum by Jay Whittaker................................198
THE CONTRIBUTORS 201
THE EDITORS..209

CONTENT WARNINGS INDEX

Assault
Queer the screen II
Are You Lonesome Tonight?
Abolish the Police
Stranger Blood is Sweeter
daughters of god

Deadnaming
Adjustment Period

Death
Jellyfish
Abolish the Police
Smudged
Titan Arum

Homophobia
Jellyfish
301.4157
Borrowed Trouble
Not This Again

Racism
Ancestry
daughters of god

Sexual Abuse
daughters of god

Suicide
Jellyfish

Surgery
Free Nipple Graft Technique

Garry Mac

FOREWORD: BENDING TIME

Positioning queerness in time is a creative act.

Often, queer people are where we are not spoken of. History is replete with erasure: closets, lacunas and gaps. We have no exodus or diaspora, nothing to tie together our collective reality. We are always new; each generation must necessarily create itself out of whole cloth. At least, so it was until the first brick was thrown at Stonewall by Marsha P. Johnson. Or Stormé DeLarverie. Or Sylvia Rivera.

Or was it before then, when authors like Woolf and Wilde performed queer narratives sub rosa, escaping the ever-present policeman's gaze of heteronormativity?

Perhaps our emergence from latency began even further back than that? Looking back into the past, we can find ourselves in those ephemeral traces, not a linear narrative but a fractured, fragmented existence, struggling to make itself known.

But when it comes to queer history, reliability and authenticity are less important than the narrative into which we write ourselves. When the individual takes up the task of rewriting state historicity, we find power in our pen. Whether we're actively oppressed by the State, society or the internal policeman installed in our heads, queerness has historically been an existence that pushes at the boundaries of what is allowed.

With gatekeepers on every side, simply existing in space can be an act of resistance; making decisions for ourselves becomes a revolutionary activity. Interrogating sex, gender and romantic attraction changes you on a subatomic level; remakes you from the ground up.

Peeking behind the curtain of dominant cultural narratives reveals a wrinkled, grey and naked conjuror, shitting on a golden throne, wanking into his own shadow, tricking us into believing he has power.

Once the magical techniques are revealed, it's impossible to fall for the illusion, to return to a binary life. Yet, it is equally impossible to escape the fact that we live within those dominant narratives. Theory alone is not a powerful enough magic with which to bring those structures down.

There is, however, a spell written into the fabric of the curtain:

'Those who cannot remember the past are condemned to repeat it.'

This spell is designed to keep us locked into the circularity of the present, and such reliance on an imagined past is at the root of many violent ideologies, bolsters ideas of supremacy, and stunts our growth. Unless we can imagine a better future, we are doomed to history.

If that thought feels too heavy, take heart; intrinsically linked to the queer mode of being beyond time is the notion of queer futurity.

To paraphrase Jack Halberstam, our entire relationship with time is strange, imaginative and eccentric. Queer time is not the same as linear, reproductive time. Without the milestones of birth, adolescence, marriage, child rearing, work, retirement, death, each of our lives become fragmented on the individual level, a microcosm of our fractured collective history.

Such fragmentation need not be a chronic source of trauma, with its attendant nihilism. Instead, it offers us the possibility of reframing ourselves in the present, standing on a horizon of becoming, looking towards a future that is not fractured, but full of fractal potential.

Freed from the constraints of linear time, we instead find ourselves unbound, existing in potentia. Unbound from time, we are free to make ourselves into whatever we wish. Will becomes the sole drive, the will-to-become.

Without societal expectations and conditions, queerness is a technology of the future; we are that which is not here yet. Utopia may seem like an unrealistic pipe dream if one belongs to linear time; but it can also serve as a direction that is otherwise difficult to describe. It is the act of facing the future. Allowing ourselves to become what we see is the supreme performance of futurition.

To face that future, we need to investigate our presence in the ephemeral past, and make space for ourselves in the present.

Our existence today is privileged because, perhaps for the first time in recorded civilisation, our lives are indelibly stamped on culture. Complexifying media and the rise of the internet has allowed us to form countless, interconnected rhizomes of recognition. Those of us who work in cultural production are telling stories, openly and without fear of censure. Those narratives are increasing in quantity and scope, and they have worked their way into the fabric of the dominant narrative so well they are now difficult to unpick. In other words, we have reached a tipping point.

It may in fact be impossible to erase us from historicity -in-the-making.

It is not in homogeneity, but in this diversity (that much-maligned word) that evolution thrives. What we do with that visibility, and the power we derive from it, may depend in part on which direction we are facing. If we turn ourselves from the past to face the future, what utopias might we begin to imagine?

★★★

José Esteban Muñoz argued in *Cruising Utopia: The Then and There of Queer Futurity* that queer futurity 'illuminates a landscape of possibility for minoritarian subjects through the aesthetic-strategies for surviving and imagining utopian modes of being in the world.' Such transgressive and creative acts of imagination can be found most in cultural production, not merely in academic theory.

The anthology you're about to lovingly break the back of is one such timely piece of cultural production, pushing at its seams with eccentric notions of time and the pure ontological joy of owning our space and being here. It is thrilling to read a collection of diverse queer voices and themes, not drawn together to *talk about queerness*, but to *talk queerly*. To tell queer stories in the here and now, that stamp their perspectives ineradicably on the dominant narrative of the present.

Inside, you'll find filmmakers struggle to piece together the celluloid history of such a diverse group of people, leaving gaps in the reel to stand in for those voices erased by censorship and historicity. Fragmented poetry reads more like fractal holography, shimmering in gel-coloured lights, while victimised 'faggots' invert the void within them and elongate, blossoming into something bigger than anyone could imagine.

Boundary dissolution thrives within, too; queer love is often a complex series of interpersonal transactions that weave between wanting to be with someone, wanting to be someone, or wanting them to absorb you, wholesale, and fix the broken parts of you. Or of transcending material love entirely, merging into pure consciousness and experiencing union. And, so, we have stories of relationships that flit between platonic connection and desire, love that thrives in its forbidden nature, love as worship; of the self, of others, of queerness itself.

There are dark and dangerous narratives here, too: excavations in the footnotes of queer history, private grief and shame shared publicly (reparation-in-progress) and reports from the frontlines where queerness violently intersects with normativity.

Poetry transcends slogans, ripping them apart and making them into a creative act of resistance.

And, here and there, hints of glimmers of that fractal queer futurity, that not-yet-here sense of surfing the peripheria of time.

More than anything, though, this anthology is the sum of all its parts; there's a rhythm here that allows each discrete unit to become part of an undulating whole.

You'll read it, and not question the identity of the authors, nor feel the need to establish their queer credentials, because the queerness within is not just in the narratives, but in the experience of reading. The shared connection between you as reader and the many writers contained within is a glittering empathetic echo of the collectivity that is required for any hope of a queer future.

Swim in it; let it fill you with light.

Put down the book, once complete, and walk away energised, queer creative juices flowing, eager to contribute your refrain to the greater song of queer experience, through the power in your pen. A song that, in this book, is thrilling, enthralling, compelling, uplifting, bittersweet, chaotic, beautiful and diverse; complex enough to be profoundly queer, and never worrying about being representative.

Read it and recognise that we were always here, and you are here, now, and so are they, and we are all in this, here, together.

Heather Valentine

PROJECTOR

The film flies through Angie's cotton-gloved hands, disappearing into the reel. Cut three. She turns the canister, positions it to feed into the projector. Molly sits in the computer chair, white fingers twisted through long brown hair, round glasses illuminated bluish-white by the first flash of pre-film.

Black and white pictures move across the makeshift screen, a bright square on bare wall. Angie moves to sit on the desk with her back to it.

She's getting sick of seeing them.

The room is quiet apart from the click of the projector, making her own silence awkward. She glances at the back of Molly's head, catching the film in the process. Two classically beautiful women run on the beach, laughing, one of them holding a length of light fabric above her head that blows in the wind. Angie looks away until the room turns dark, and clicks the projector off.

'It's… nice,' Molly offers as she turns the lights back on.

'Nice?' Angie replies.

Molly turns her head. 'It's not a very Angie film, is it?'

Angie slumps, still sitting against the desk. 'The brief said *celebrates*. Use material from the from the Pink Pictures archive to create a short film that *celebrates* LGBT film history.'

'So you made some twee bollocks,' Molly says.

'So I made some twee bollocks,' Angie sighs.

Molly turns around to face her, leaning her bony arms on the back of the chair. 'It needs to be a bit more punk, yeah?'

Angie nods, then shakes her head. 'But it's this uplifting shit that goes viral.' And she lifts her hands to gesture around the room. 'I'm not going to be able to use this after I graduate. I can't rent this shit myself. I need to start making things people want to watch. Autostraddle left *Monster* out of its *Top 100 Lesbian Films* because it was too depressing. I can't just be my depressing self. It's not what people want.'

Molly shrugs. 'I mean, I guess it's a response to the mainstream media, dead lesbians etcetera. Radical positivity.'

'Is twee bollocks still radical?' Angie asks, raising an eyebrow. 'I mean, which is it?

'You know it's complicated,' Molly replies. 'But I was devil's advocating there, sorry. Not helpful.'

Reels and reels of Angie's rejects sit in her locker. Collages of Italian horror movies, lurid blood-stained murderesses, loving tributes to bisexual psychopaths and lesbian predators, re-cutting scenes of knife-crazy trans women to remove double-takes in horror or amusement and leave them as powerful, nasty and vulnerable as the dark-haired male villains that big-hearted teenage girls grab on to. No nice people. Real messy mental queers like her, real out of control screaming like she is when she has an episode.

Thank you for your submission, but it's not quite what we're looking for.

'Besides, you know what else I'm going to say,' Molly says.

And Angie does. 'It's all bourgeoisie white cis lesbians, and I shouldn't sell that to people as queer history even if that's what they want.'

Molly smiles awkwardly. Yeah, it was that. 'There were a couple bourgeoisie white cis men for variety,' she adds.

'I'll see what I can do before the deadline to fix some of that,' Angie says. But if she can't, this is how it's going in. 'Anyway.'

Molly reaches for her bag. Angie reaches for the keys to lock up.

'I'll walk you home, yeah?' Angie says. Molly smiles, drawing up to her full height. Angie flicks the last light off as they leave, and shuts the door on the studio.

Angie can't sleep again. She finds herself up at four in the morning, hunched over her laptop on her bed and flicking through the Pink Pictures archive again.

They said LGBT film history, and they meant history alright. A lot of the films in the archive are Hays Code, pre-Stonewall, however you like to put it. All subtext. She can look at a film and feel that someone is bisexual like her, but how can she make an audience who isn't looking see that reality?

Marlene Dietrich? Molly's voice says in her head. Marlene Dietrich's films are still in copyright and the archive is all UK films, so she isn't there and she can't add her in. There isn't a lot she can do about the whiteness with what she has, either — the early African-American film pioneers she knows from class are, well, American.

Either way, she makes gaps for them. In the cut four file, deleting some of the tamer glamour shots. Pulling apart seconds to put herself in.

Some of the subtext films have hetero pairings in them, she could cut around them with actresses that look similar. The short, amateur, real collection gems don't, so there isn't a lot to work with there. A few people in androgynous style, a handful of drag queens, and the films are from a time when that could have meant they were trans. Or it could not.

Her hands fly across the keys, pinching clips. Then they stop. A collage can bring out subtext and make it text. Or it can make text appear that isn't there. Is she doing bisexuals like her or trans women like Molly a disservice if she tricks them into thinking the films in this archive have something in it they don't?

It's why she shied away from touching the edgier films, and dove more into the identity politics heartwarming angle.

Because there were about three experimental films that still hold up and at that point she might as well have just copied them and sent them in as her entry.

What she's looking for isn't here. What's here is two handsome men, two pretty women, being gently queer. And she's sure there are ways in which that is still radical, but not with her. That's the starting line to her. Watching nice films over and over again isn't her. Watching films just for their representation isn't good enough. She wants to feel the ground break beneath her feet.

Celebrate isn't the problem. It's that what she wants to celebrate is invisible.

There has to be a queer female Derek Jarman, Jean Cocteau, Kenneth Anger, Oscar Micheaux. A queer female Stanley Kubrick, Dario Argento, Bill Gunn, Quentin Tarantino, even.

She has to be out there, waiting to be celebrated, and Angie just hasn't found her yet.

Angie starts up the file-to-reel she borrowed from the studio. She prints her new cut, same length, black holes where her history should be. She already feels guilty, like she always does when she goes too far. It's a waste of film, she's never going to send this cut in. She'll screen it for Molly, yell a bit and then send in the twee bollocks because the deadline is next week and she has classwork to do too.

Maybe this isn't a very Angie project, then, she imagines Molly saying. But she can't expect to only do things that are perfect for her if she wants to be a professional. She doesn't stop the reel.

Maybe she should have stitched together the lying cut. She works on it while she waits for Molly to arrive. Keeping herself busy. The film is already in the last projector that was free, chairs pulled up. Maybe she can cut together speeches to the camera, insert a sexual ambiguity through the meta-knowledge that the audience could be of any gender or identity.

The door opens and Molly comes in, hands fussing with her satchel strap.

'Molly, I'm going off track again,' Angie says.

'Alright,' Molly replies.

'Is it still a celebration of LGBT history if I'm basically making a new film?'

'Not really, no,' Molly says, hanging her brown faux-suede coat on the back of the door. 'Maybe keep that for another submission.'

'Right, thanks.'

Molly crosses the room towards the seat closest to Angie. 'Is this on track?' she asks, gesturing at the projector.

Angie shakes her head, then shrugs. 'I don't know. It might be. I don't think so. I wanted to show you anyway.' She catches Molly's eyes as she props her glasses up. 'I think it's good. I need to make sure it makes sense outside of my head.'

'Okay, I'll try and figure it out,' Molly replies.

Angie clicks the light off, and the projector on. The same twee bollocks opening scene, a classic beautiful shop assistant looking longingly at a classic beautiful rich woman leaving the store. The first blank. She looks away again. If Molly doesn't like it, she doesn't want to see it on her face.

The projector rattles, and to Angie's ears makes a worrying noise. She turns around to see it approaching another gap. The projector goes dark. Flicker flicker, filaments of light dance in her darkness, shapes like figures.

'Oh, fuck,' Angie mutters. The filmstock must be damaged. She must have grabbed a faulty canister, maybe touched it somehow.

'What?' Molly says, turning to look during the next twee bollocks sequence.

'They're supposed to be blanks,' Angie says.

Molly opens her mouth to answer, then turns back to the projector at another stretch of darkness. The streaks of light come back, and like clouds she imagines she can see them in more detail, make out hands and mouths.

'No, this is better,' Angie says, as the beach women sequence plays again. 'They're like — the ghosts of films that should have been.'

The last normal sequence plays out, and the projector flickers into a few last seconds of darkness, the lights seeming to get brighter. Then the projector stops.

'It's like what you say about your horror films, and your collages. It's taking subtext and making it into something real.' Angie smiles as Molly continues. 'Like, uh, Lovecraft and depression.'

'Hey, keep that racist clown out of my studio,' Angie laughs.

'Like Poe and — oh wait, slavery apologist,' Molly replies.

'Like the Vincent Price film versions of Lovecraft and Poe's books,' Angie suggests.

'Yes, he's an angel,' Molly grins, before her eyes fall back upon the projector. 'But anyway — yes. You'll need to foreground it for someone who doesn't know what your angle is. *Celebrating queer history from the archive, and mourning queer history that was lost.* It might not be right for this sub if you're sure it's a twee bollocks sub. But it's good.'

'It's good to hear you say that,' Angie says. 'And I like your subtitle, I'm stealing that.' She can take this to class, ask her professor for advice on turning it into something original. She begins to dismantle the projector set-up, moves to pack up the film reel.

'You're welcome to it,' Molly says. 'Anyway, it's your turn now. Let me just boot up my laptop and I'll show you my new draft.'

Angie smiles vacantly at the space on the wall where her film was, as Molly rustles in her bag. When she blinks it's almost painful. As if they're still shining there, the dancing shapes emerge against her eyelids, burning green and blue.

* * *

The twee bollocks reel lies on Angie's desk, packaged up and labelled for Pink Pictures. She sits on her bed, eyes towards the ceiling, where blue speckles still glitter in her vision. Aching, throbbing. She is putting this down to some sort of dehydration, eyes strained from computer light and the dryness of the projector rooms.

She turns back to her laptop anyway, hands moving without thought, following her instincts as the shapes seem to float behind this file or that. Looking for pieces of her original vision, still half-wondering if she can pull out a better version of her submission in time, splice in Molly's subtitle and send the ghost version in.

The sound of someone else coming into the dorm. Angie glances away, and when she turns back she's lost. She can't make sense of what she's chosen. She looks through her notes, as if waking up from a dream and trying to remember it. Seeing the phrase *heighten the melodrama* and not being sure what she meant or how she meant to go about doing that when she wrote it down.

Angie puts the laptop on the floor and lies back. That turn her brain can put on her, the head-tiredness, the nausea and the anger, flows at the edges of her mind. She's at the point where she can still notice them. When she crosses the line, she won't even realise. Rubs her eyes with her palms, and the pain splits her skull, a line across the top of her head from the base of her neck to between her eyebrows. Her whole vision filling with a multi-coloured burn, a shape like a face emerging in the middle, still the colour of her eyelids. She isn't scared. She's annoyed. Tries to hold on to Molly's praise, pull herself back, but it slips. Just restlessness, and itchy hands.

Too early, not enough sleep, Angie comes back into the studio, rucksack full of reels, the disintegrating film hot against her shoulders. Finds a room, sets up a projector. Lets it play. The shapes grow larger, brighter. The tears don't just stay in the darkness now, they cut across the archive tapes. Blotting out the actresses, seeming to create other figures.

The film flies through Angie's cotton-gloved hands, as she sets it back to the start.

Her first clips have almost completely gone now. Only the classic beautiful shop assistant remains, shakily moving through the light. *She also wrote social-realist screenplays, but they were never produced.* In the blanks, daguerreotype sketches of unknown films, strange women in occult costumes in one reel, throbbing neon modernism in the next. *Screened at local film festivals, but never picked up.* The light crawls, the walls cracking and splitting, the way it feels like her head is. She can barely feel anything other than the pain now, is vaguely aware that her fingertips are moving to touch the projector controls, until all her peripheral vision is filled with the multi-coloured light.

A cooling sensation like water, fingers brushing her eyes shut.

'Why do you think it hurts, Angie?' A soft, husky voice.

'I don't know,' Angie replies.

'The same way it hurts when you have been sleeping, and someone turns on the light.'

The pressure releases from her head. Angie opens her eyes. She sees, in flickering technicolour, a woman standing in front of her. Through an archway behind her, a scene of theme park Grecian paradise, blurry like the last surviving set photo of something lost. Plaster props, all sorts of people behind her dressed in costume.

'It's like the ghost,' Angie murmurs. 'Of the films that should have been.'

'There's no should have,' the woman replies. 'Only have. You are not building a first. You are building on the rich tapestry of the hidden world. This is reality, Angie.'

Her film flickers through her eyes, imprinted in double over the paradise set. Some of the women, some of the drag queens, some of the androgynous dressers lit up in a blue-green halo. Her reject reels, the horror films and the strange experiments she's watched, woven with their own filaments. The daguerreotypes, flashes of strange visions. The fault line she's been feeling for, films that make friction.

'Some people are not interested in seeing reality. They paper over it, obscure it, pretend that there is nothing beyond what survives. Did the Celts have no inner life, because it is not written down? No. Is your history not real, because it is harder to find? No.'

Angie nods.

'We bless you, strange angel, with the secret world's sight. You will recognise what has been hidden from you, you will be drawn to your invisible kind. Your obligation, now, is to weave. Is to make yourself visible, so that your artistic descendants may see. Take from them the burden you carry, of a nostalgia for an unknown past.'

'I understand,' Angie says. The woman touches her forehead, parts her fingers, opening a third eye.

Find them, not just because they're like her. Find them, these traditions buried and lost, because they are great lost works, surviving only in the hearts of those who had the fortune to see them.

There is a knock on the door. Angie stirs in her chair, the room back to normal, as if waking from a dream. The projector is still loaded, the reel at an end.

The door opens, and Molly enters. Blazing with a green halo, turned pastel and gentle, nourishing rather than painful to the eyes.

'Hey, you didn't say what room to find you in,' she says.

Angie doesn't remember calling, but knows she must have. She walks over to the projector, switching it for her updated reel, the ghostly tears re-appearing as a soft glow. Cut five. She loads it, the subtitle borrowed from Molly first.

'Thanks for coming,' Angie says. 'There aren't a lot of changes, but I wanted you to see.'

'Oh, sure thing,' Molly replies.

Pulling the thread, feeling for the edge. Vincent Price's creature in the pit, always lurking but only now visible. The multi-coloured light, pulsing from her heart. More than human, like the beautiful monsters that dark-hearted girls like Molly write poems to

She also wrote social-realist screenplays, but they were never produced. Screened at local film festivals, but never picked up. A limited run of 300 DVDs. She submitted her work under a false name, and could never be tracked down.

Angie didn't know where this would end up, but she could feel a first step. A first clue, a re-discovery, of these artists long buried alive.

AR Crow

QUEER THE SCREEN II

The urgency of the disco beat
        the heartbeat
                the fight
                        the fucking

  when no-one knows how long it can keep going

        how long any of this can keep going

                or who will get beaten next.

KATY PERRY REMIX

I kissed a gay guy and he liked it

Amidst queer adolescence
　　the taste of validation
is stronger, sweeter
　　than any Jägerbomb

I lost my stuff then found it again
I lost myself then found him again

Jane Flett

JELLYFISH

Leah started calling me Jellyfish because of the tattoo. She says that's what it looks like — a big amorphous blob, all head and no heart. It's her fault. It was supposed to be an actual heart, an extra one for the outside, because my first was all bunged up from not enough kissing.

I try, I try. I do. But there's no one in this school both willing and worthy for these lips.

Anyway, after two-thirds of a bottle of Malibu, Leah's hand was less steady than my own pounding chest, and the heart came out how it came out. She says I should be grateful. She read on the internet that mixing glitter with tattoo ink is a recipe for infection, septic sores, and skin cancer. She read it after we did it. You can't really see the glitter sparkling under the skin, but the lines healed up well enough.

So Jellyfish is better than a septic sore. And sometimes, when I'm lying in bed at night, waiting for the suburbs to come down and crush me, I run my fingers over my second heart and whisper Jellyfish, Jellyfish, Jellyfish.

I feel my own tentacles wriggle, and I know I'll get out of here soon.

The name caught on because people do what Leah says. She may not be in the cool clique, but she terrifies them, which is better. She brings a three-inch blade to biology and runs it up and down the inside of her calf when Mrs Massie's not paying attention, holding the eyes of anyone who dares look at her the way a lioness might hold a kitten in her jaws. Her locker door is covered in Catholic iconography and crusted tampons nailed up with drawing pins. If anyone asks why, she says 'spellwork' and does that grin that shows all the way to her molar gold.

It's because of her I get beaten up half as much as I used to. It's because of her Jellyfish has replaced faggot as the nom du jour. We have a special relationship, one based in effigies of Marilyn Monroe, the Devil tarot card from the Raider-Smith-White deck, and a predilection for hardcore BDSM chatrooms.

'Go on, go on, tell him you're fourteen,' she gasps, as I have the forty-eight-year-old stockbroker eating out of the filthy dogbowl of my hand. 'Tell him you're a boy.'

Sometimes I think she keeps me around because I am the most imaginative pervert she could find. Her own descriptions always fall flat, always stutter into some inane loop-the-loop of put it in, put it in again, hey keep putting it in and out and in again.

'*Not* a boy,' I say, and I tell the man I've lifted my tartan skirt up around the pudgy white flesh of my stomach. I say I'm holding the crucifix tight in my hand, the bulldog clips clamped tight on my poor innocent nipples. I describe the texture of the lard waiting by my twinkling pink asshole.

< I could put it in now. If you like? I'm a bit nervous :) >

No matter how Leah pleads, I refuse to use text speak beyond the occasional emoticon.

'It's more real!' she says. 'It's what they expect.'

But even I'm not that perverse.

The truth is I love it as much as she does. Together we're glamour whores and magicians, clad in sparkly rags and filthy intent. Through the internet, we can make anyone do anything. Take an old man and unwrap him and force everything we want into the dark passages that lurk in his own sack of skin.

< I'm tugging on the bulldog clip. It hurts . . . >

< thinking about how it would feel if it was your cock this

sharp in my ass >

< oh ow. oh my god. ow.! >

That's when he disconnects. They all disconnect sooner or later, because someone's got to come first, and it's not going to be us, giggling and passing the cheap red wine bottle between us, our lips purple and hilarious.

'Some people have no staying power,' she says, and I agree.

Even though I'm protected at school by Leah's magical cloak, it's not always effective. This isn't her fault. It's mine, because sometimes I bore of safe spaces. Or rather, it's because sometimes Joe Shearer's tighter-than-tight jeans are a miracle of denim-skin-particle-physics, and who among us has never felt the desire to call him Princess, to tell him we're duty bound to pick up whatever he's putting down?

That is why I end up in the locker.

My left leg is bent up awkwardly and my cheekbone is tight and swollen where Joe's fist made contact, but it was worth it for the moment our eyes met and I called him Bambi. Bambi and Jellyfish: a love story for the ages, even if he hasn't come to terms with it yet. There's a chance the cheekbone will turn into a black eye, and then I'll be like Patti Smith pretending to be Anouk Aimée, and no one will be able to resist me: not now, not a bit, not ever.

I just need to get out of here first.

Squirming my hips, I jiggle my leg so I'm half-kneeling, and reach my hand around. If I can get the catch in my hand, I'll swipe it up and be gone. A regular Houdini (who, let's face it, had a soft spot for the old handcuffs himself). So I wriggle and I squeeze, and that does it: the door clangs open and I topple out elegantly like a Russian teen gymnast, head over fucking heels.

I'm about to slam the door behind me when I notice my hand-painted goth phase Justin Bieber poster is starting to peel away from the metal, a tragic side-effect of sweat and BluTac, undoubtedly. My hand is poised by Justin's adorable baby goth raccoon eyes, ready to tack it back, when something stops me. There, right at the spot where Justin is peeling away.

Something? No. Nothing. A gaping nothingness, a thing without things, a place without *stuff* in the place. I remove the poster, and there it is beneath. A perfectly rectangular A4 abyss, just the size of Justin, waiting for me.

'Hello?' I whisper, and my voice immediately stretches out long and tacky, chewing gum between flip flops and hot tarmac. 'Hellooooooooooooo?'

I shudder, I slam the door shut. I'm still holding Justin. He looks up, all helpless innocent babyface, as the O of my hello echoes foreverly down that endless metal canal.

'Shh!' I hiss, and the H of my shh sucks into the locker too, bouncing off the O to make an inhale-exhale, 'Oh-huh-oh-huh-oh-huh.'

My mouth is ready to shriek 'Fuck!' and it is only by the clamp of my darling manicured fingers that it does not.

Instead, I open the locker again. Slowly. I take a pencil from my backpack and I poke the abyss with the tip, though even as I do it I'm thinking what are you doing, Jellyfish? Why this reaction, faced with something you don't understand, to give it a wee poke?

There's a sharp tug, and I grab the pencil tighter, and then a rattling noise, the accidental inhale of a penny in the hoover. When I pull the pencil out it is entirely hollow. The lead swallowed. And with that I pull my finger back, the one which was stretching to follow.

Instead, I line up Justin very perfectly with the edges of the hole, like a lid. It seems like the right thing to do. The edges flipper-flapper for a moment but then they settle, tight, against the wall of the locker. If you didn't know anything was behind it, you wouldn't guess a thing.

I sling my bag on my back. It's too late for class now, so I go to sit in our spot — The Hole — round the back of Asda by the bins with all filthiest graffiti, and I wait for her to get out too.

'I have something important to tell you,' I say grandly, as Leah clambers into The Hole.

'He said *yes*?' Her mouth says it though her face doesn't believe it. Then she leans in close and draws one highlighter yellow fingernail across my cheekbone. 'And then you consummated it like this?'

'Ow!' I yelp. 'No.' I smooth down the white pleather of my skirt and look around for the right words to explain. 'There's a hole in my locker.'

'Dear Liza, Dear Liza,' she sings.

'I'm serious! It sucked the lead right out of my pencil.'

I manage to maintain my Very Serious expression for ten more seconds before we both collapse into giggles.

'That's handy,' she says. 'Since I'm guessing Joe's not going to be doing that any time soon.'

I let out a long pfffft. 'Babe, I'm serious. I think it's some kind of magic. Just think of all the things we can do with it.'

'Come on then.' Leah's tone is conciliatory, although her mouth is still bunched up in a little smirk. 'Let us see.'

Staring at the abyss, I can't think of a single thing to do with it. We now have two leadless pencils and three inkless pens and no way of taking notes in biology.

'If you lined a zit up just right,' she says, fingering her chin. 'Then—' and she makes a big slurping sound, the sound of spaghetti ricocheting between a slack pair of lips.

'Gross.'

'Chuck your homework in here.' She grins, her gold tooth glinting. 'Tell Mrs Massie the void ate it.'

I roll my eyes. 'As if.'

'Or maybe it's an escape hatch,' she suggests, leaning back against the lockers and drumming the metal with her heel. 'Maybe it's your secret way out of here.'

To this, I don't say anything. I'm thinking of the spell I did two nights ago, the one with the spit on my windowpane and the magic mantra. What it means when I say Jellyfish in bed at night. Because that's what it is, isn't it? A wriggly thing, one that can scooch out of trouble when need be. Jellyfish aren't stuck with bones or brains, keeping them stuck to things that are no good.

But then again, I'm not ready to end up like that pencil. So I close the locker door. I laugh and say I'll think about it.

I do; I can't stop thinking about it.

Is it my stop to get off or the end of the line?

A week passes. The abyss is there, still, at the edge of my thoughts and the tips of my fingers, but my skin and guts remain united. For now at least. I do my best to ignore it while I figure things out, but one afternoon between classes, when no one is looking, I peel Justin back and flick a photo of Jayne Mansfield inside.

Somehow I've got it in my head that the abyss — or Justin's Void, as I've secretly rechristened her — is hungry. I can't tell if it's because she's been sending me secret psychic pleas whenever I open the locker door. Or maybe it's just that I was brought up Catholic, so my reaction to anything holy is to get on my knees and start making offerings.

In a millisecond, Jayne is gone, and I close the locker door to press my forehead against it.

'Taking a nap?'

I turn to see Leah grinning behind me, picking at a bloody scab on her arm. I laugh, I'm about to tell her about the hunger, when something catches in my throat and I don't. Somehow, it feels like my secret, our secret, mine and that glorious gaping hole.

'Give us a go,' I say instead, and I wiggle my pink fingernail at her scab.

'Shut up you gobshite,' she says, and we walk down the corridor arm in arm.

Before too long, the abyss starts showing up in our chatroom sessions too. Innocently at first — as innocent as you can get in the midst of this anyway. It's no leap from St Andrew's Crosses to me asking

< do you want to stretch me out? >

and the response is yes, yes he does. But something else sneaks in to my fingers and what comes out is

< now suck out my insides >

and he doesn't type anything at all after that for a while.

< elongate my nipples >

< suck me traverse the space time continuum stick it in my infinite void hole >

I feel like a bot that's been set up to play chess but got distracted on the way by filth. Our man disconnects, and Leah tells me I'm going weird. She's one to talk though, she's started reading cannibal snuff cartoons, the ones where the blonde girls end up skewered for the barbecue and loving it.

'I don't get it,' she says, tapping a finger on the keyboard. 'I mean I'd eat it, totals, but why would you want to die like that?'

I peer over her shoulder to her screen, where a pair of huge-breasted twins are squealing over a butcher's hook.

'I guess it's one way to live forever,' I reply.

Back at school, I start slipping the abyss everything I think she would like: single serving sachets of lube, gold lamé nail polish, last February's issue of *Scream Queen* magazine, the one with the free 3D glasses and squirts-out-of-ten decapitation ratings. I don't question my action; it's the right thing to do.

She swallows it all with the same carefree gulp.

At night, I close up all the windows and let it reach a high pitch of sweaty intensity. As my skin turns slick, then dripping, I wrap a scarf in my hand and imagine it is Joe Shearer's basketball shorts, sleek and slippery. I close my eyes and tug at my cock, and things stretch out long and infinite. It's my own fist at my throat when I come, but it's Joe's too, and the void's on top of that.

Nothing is quite so simple and straightforward as it's made out to be, except the next day, when I slink the lavender silk into the hole, and it is.

'Hey Bambi,' I whisper as Joe walks past, and a mottled red creeps up the back of his neck.

'Fuck you, faggot,' he says.

'It's Jellyfish,' I say to my locker door. 'Jellyfish and Bambi.'

There is a long pause, the sound of an invisible boundary snapping.

'What did you say?' He coughs it out, like it's a line he's been waiting for. 'What the fuck did you fucking say?'

That's when things start to happen in slow motion. I've seen enough Gregg Araki movies to know what it means when things start happening in slow motion.

Joe puts his hand inside his bag and comes out with a shiny black gun. It doesn't look real. It looks like a silhouette, like someone has cut out the shape of gun in the fabric of reality and here is the black outline of what's left behind.

'Hey fucknut!' yells Leah, who is somehow here by my side. She takes a step towards me, her arms spreading.

Joe points it straight at my chest, right at the spot of my second heart.

My jellyfish.

I blink once, very slowly, still nowhere near adjusted to the facts of reality. I swoon back against my locker. I close my eyes tight.

When everyone started calling me Jellyfish, I started reading facts about them. Or rather, what I mean is when Leah started calling me Jellyfish. I read that their stinger uncoiling is one of the fastest actions in nature. That they can shoot out even faster than a bullet from a gun.

So I lean against my locker and I wait for my stingers to erupt into the afternoon, or his bullet, whatever's going to happen first. Then, when nothing happens, I peek out of one eye.

He is pointing the gun with both hands, both hands that are shaking.

I can hear my own heartbeat pounding, Oh-huh-oh-huh-oh-huh. And then I realise it's not my heartbeat anymore. It's coming from beside me, not inside. It's the abyss, my words coming back to meet me.

He is cocking the trigger.

I feel my body become something looser and longer. I'm still standing here, sure, but also there's a part of me that's elongating.

'I'm not a faggot,' Joe says, his voice getting higher and higher. His hands still shaking. 'Don't fucking talk to me.'

I want to wrap my arms around him and tell him it's okay. He doesn't have to be anything. He can be just whoever he is, and not worry anymore, and that's fine.

But I can't. It's too late. I'm already hurtling, past him, past Justin, through time and space. In the abyss, I start to glimpse the things I chucked inside. I reach out a hand and close it around a pair of diamanté bedazzled sunglasses, and I place them on my face. Scooting past my nose, a purple Rimmel lipstick. I paint my lips and blot them on the skin of my elbow.

As I fly, head over high heels through the void, I'm thinking about the movies. About *The Wizard of Oz*, mainly, and how that was supposed to be a happy ending. They say there's no place like home but I'm not sure that means much, I'm not sure it's a selling point. Because who'd choose home over the Emerald City? Who wants sepia when you could be existing in Technicolor?

Me, I'm waiting for my heart to split open and rain red cardboard cutouts all over the corridor floor. I'm waiting to bash up against something strange and impossible.

I spread my arms, and I twist towards the light.

Gray Crosbie

ADJUSTMENT PERIOD

in my throat
I deepen the words
'Soy caramel latte —
to take away'
I pay
step aside
wait

not realising my mistake
until they've called on me
three times
(at least)

and hand me the paper cup
scrawled
with permanent ink

my birth name
scalding my hand

Christina Neuwirth

SEQUINS

The first time Robyn invited me round I must have been about twelve or thirteen. I distinctly remember it because she normally asked a group of us to come over, but this particular time she only asked me. She said, 'What are you doing after swimming on Thursday?'

'My Mum is picking me up.'

'You could come home with me and we could pick out summer camps in the brochure my dad got.'

'Okay,' I said. I didn't want to ask further questions because I was worried it might scare Robyn off.

That night it was hard to get to sleep after dinner. I couldn't stop thinking about the next day.

After school, Robyn and I walked to swimming together. Heather was there too, and Robyn was talking to her. She hadn't really looked at me all day, not since I'd told her that I was allowed to come over — she'd said 'Fun!' and then proceeded to ignore me. I was used to it, but it still tied my stomach into knots.

Heather and Robyn giggled and splashed around the shallow end of the pool while the rest of us did our warm-up laps. Miss Feever told them off, but then concentrated more on timing the rest of us on our butterfly laps.

Robyn didn't even look at me.

I had brought a change of clothes but Robyn always left

quickly after training so I knew better than to try and get completely cleaned up and changed now. She was wrapped in a towel and smiling when I came out of the changing rooms with my bag and my dripping hair.

'Quick, let's get to mine,' she said.

'Yes.' I wasn't sure if we were back to being friendly so I figured I'd better stay quiet for another little while. In the car, her mum asked us a few questions but Robyn was always quicker to answer. It was only a ten-minute drive. At the end of it I felt suddenly cold in my stomach. I checked the time. It was three. I was meant to be home by seven.

When we arrived, Robyn ran to the bathroom and I could hear the shower through the closed door. Robyn's mum kept asking me questions in the front room. I sat on the edge of the sofa.

When Robyn was done she came out wrapped in a number of big towels. Steam drifted from the open door of the bathroom into the hallway.

'What are you waiting for?' asked Robyn and called me to her room. 'Are you not going to shower?' she said without looking at me.

'Um.' I didn't know what the right thing was.

'You know you need to shower every day now. Leave it any longer than that and you'll start to smell, like Gary.'

'Of course. I'm going to shower,' I said. 'Can I shower here?'

'Of course, silly! That's why I asked. Ask mum for a towel, we've got loads — they're so soft. Much softer than the ones at your house, I bet!' said Robyn. She'd never even been to mine.

Their bathroom was huge. It had a shower and a tub, separate, and a warming towel rack. I put the towel Robyn's mum had given me on the rack. It was turquoise and extremely fluffy. I took my clothes off, folded them, and put them on a little wicker stool by the sink. Then I got into the shower and turned the tap on. There were several big bottles of shampoo and shower gel in there, and I used small amounts and took care to put them back facing the right way. I tried to do everything as quickly as possible. I didn't want to take too long, but I also didn't want Robyn to think I wasn't showering properly. I wiped the floor of the shower with my feet to get rid of any hairs I might have left behind, and dried myself off, then put on my clothes again. I felt better.

Robyn met me outside the bathroom and said, 'That took forever. What makes you think you can use up all our hot water?'

'I don't know.'

'What?' She came closer.

'I'm sorry.'

'Maggie, darling?' Robyn's mum interrupted. 'Are you staying for dinner?'

I didn't know what to say. I wanted to leave. I wanted, desperately, to not be rude.

'Of course she's staying!' said Robyn, her face suddenly kind again, throwing her arm around my shoulder and pulling my head closer until it touched the side of hers. She didn't mind that my hair was wet, or that I had used a lot of hot water to get clean. Her arm around my shoulder felt warm and soft.

Robyn grabbed my hand and we went to her room. When we were there I asked if I could phone home to let my Mum know I was staying for dinner. She said I didn't need to do that, and that using the phone would cost money. Then she said we should both cut our hair.

'It would be so cool! We could both have the same haircut. My mum cuts my hair all the time. It's easy.'

She said the best way to cut hair was to tie it into two pigtails and then snip them off. She tied up her hair first: it was long and ginger and still damp. It smelled lovely. I wondered if she could smell her shampoo on me. She brushed my hair very carefully with a large-toothed comb. It was long and bushy, and normally my Mum and I would detangle it as quickly as possible, which always resulted in tears and shouting. When Robyn did it, it didn't hurt at all. She was very careful. Then she tied it into pigtails. We looked cute already, and the same, which made me feel warm and gooey. She stood me up and we looked at ourselves and each other in her full-length mirror.

'I'll get the scissors. This is going to be so fun!' she said. She arrived back with the pointy hairdressing scissors, which were packed in a plastic case that said they were indeed made for that purpose.

'Shall I go first? Or do you want to?' she asked. She unzipped the case, took out the scissors, opened them and held them to her pigtails.

'Um,' I said.

'I can go first if you're scared!' she said, and gripped her own pigtails.

'No, it's ok, I'm not scared.'

I cut off my pigtails.

She didn't cut off hers.

That was the first time I was round at Robyn's.

I arrive at the venue and I know she'll be here. It would've been weird if Jenni hadn't invited her. We are all each other's friends, after all. I try not to crane my head in case it's too obvious, but I want to see her before she sees me. There aren't many people here — it's still early. I know Jenni wouldn't have put me and Robyn at the same table, but I check the chart just in case. At least we won't have to watch each other eat. We won't have to make conversation over a plate of food. We won't have to clink glasses.

I still have a small hope that I will be asked to stay overnight at the hotel, even though I helped Jenni with the booking and she mentioned that those rooms are for family and out of town visitors, and that I, living 45 minutes away, can just sleep at home. I don't mind, right? I don't mind.

Robyn has a room at the hotel. So she's *out of town*, now.

My stomach is flipping.

I see Jenni has seated me next to Thomas who is recently

single, so maybe I can flirt with him and that'll distract me.

Weddings have sort of stopped being exciting after I've been to so many, of colleagues and friends and cousins, but Jenni's is different, because we've known each other for fifteen years. And because I can tell she is so happy, and Tabby is happy. They got married in the back garden this morning at 8am when the sun was still pale and the dew was still on the grass, and other romantic things like that.

'Jesus Christ, what a day,' says Jenni, rushing out of a side door and nearly running me over.

'Is everything okay?' I say.

'Yes, yes, it's fine. It's just non-stop.' She waves off my offers of help, points me to a corner where others have already left their bags and coats, and leaves me to look for my seat.

'Maggie! Hi!' says a familiar voice. I turn around and I feel my face get hot. Not her. Not yet. I scramble for the right name.

'Danielle!' I say.

We stand for a few minutes talking, but the hallway is starting to stress me out — the confined space, how exposed I am, the big poofy shoulders on my dress, so I ask her where the bathroom is.

The bathroom is cooler than the rest of the hotel. It's also surprisingly quiet. Except, there she is: Robyn.

'Oh, hi!' she says. Her hair is bobbed and more auburn than ginger now. It suits her, makes her neck look slender and elegant, swan-like. Her dress is blue, and shiny all over, and the pleats running down the side of it will look lovely when she dances.

She shows me her teeth.

Is she smiling? I can't tell.

Yes.

It's a friendly, *Oh hi.*

'Hi, Robyn! Fancy bumping into you here!' I say. It is a really weird thing to say but it is what comes out of my mouth.

'So,' she begins.

'Listen, I'm sorry, I'm bursting. Lots of tea this morning. I'll just see you in there, yeah?' I add a little laugh at the end, and she indulges me and laughs too. I push past her and into the first cubicle I can find. I sit down, but can't even start peeing until after I hear the door shut.

I try to remember whether she is angry with me, or am I angry with her? It was all such a long time ago. A searing memory of a kiss — one-sided, sloppy — comes back to me, but I push it aside.

Not now.

I remember the first time I chose my own outfit without consulting Robyn. Normally Robyn and I would be on the phone to make sure we didn't match, or to make sure that we did, but for some reason at this particular party, we hadn't. We were sixteen. I was wearing a loose-fitting black dress, with casual flare and pleating at the skirt. The top bit was covered in black sequins that were arranged to form small roses. My Mum had bought it for me and I thought I looked very casual goth. I'd put eyeliner on and pinned back my black hair.

Robyn was already at the party when I arrived. It wasn't anything fancy, just at someone's house on a Saturday, with three Bacardi Breezers to last a room full of people for the night. She was wearing jeans and a t-shirt, and I instantly realised that I was wearing the wrong thing. Some other girls were in dresses, and some of them looked more dressed up than others, but seeing Robyn there in what she was wearing, and the way she looked at me, I knew I was in trouble.

She said *Hi* like normal, and we went and got a drink and stood in a corner to assess the party situation together, and when she'd been nice to me for long enough it started.

'You're shiny today,' she said.

'Yes,' I said. I didn't even try to defend myself. I was wrong. I looked stupid.

'Did you think it was fancy dress?' she said.

'No,' I said. She was looking me full in the face, and I was looking down at my cup.

'Because we could've both dressed up as old ladies if that was the idea,' she said.

There was no use trying. I just let it wash over me.

'Listen. I can help. I have a scarf. If you wear it over your front like this, maybe — oh, shit, is it on the back too?'

I nodded as she walked around me looking at the intricate sequin roses.

'There's nothing for it. They'll have to come off.'

I looked down at my stomach, at the floral pattern.

'Come on,' she said, like we were co-conspirators. She took my hand and led me to the bathroom, where we found, after rummaging in our friend's parents' medicine cabinet, some nail scissors. They were bent to follow the curve of a fingernail.

'It'll be tricky but it'll have to do,' she said. Before she made the first cut, she tipped my face up by poking my chin with her finger. 'You're okay with this, right? I mean, you didn't want to be a shiny granny all night, did you?'

I nodded. I tried not to think about how excited both Mum and I had been when she'd bought the dress.

'Okay,' said Robyn. She giggled. She came really close to me, pulled on one of the sequins, and cut the tiny thread of stitching that connected it to the fabric of the bodice. It took a long time. There were a lot of sequin roses on that dress.

Robyn's seamstress work wasn't very accurate because the scissors were bent, so in the end I had lots of small holes all over the dress. The fabric was loose enough so they didn't show up flat against my body but I could still see them, and, standing in a circle of sequins on the bathroom tiles, I felt like she'd clipped my wings instead.

After the operation was over, Robyn and I knelt on the cold tiles together and cupped our hands to sweep up the sequins that were all over the floor. We put them in the bathroom bin, downed our sickly sweet drinks, and went back to the party. Robyn was laughing again, rubbing my back, reassuring me that the dress was great now and I looked amazing. I laughed, too.

When Mum picked me up I told her Robyn didn't like the sequins. She gave me a row, saying it didn't matter, that I should only care what I liked, but I tuned it out. I'd heard it too many times before. She didn't know anything.

I check my face, wipe the inevitable mascara smudge from the side of my eyes, and rearrange the poofy top bit of my wedding reception dress. I remind myself again that this is the dress Jenni wanted me to wear, and this day is about her. Not about impressing Robyn, or about anyone else.

I reach the hall again, which has filled with more people, so I go to my table and take a swig of water. A couple of people are sitting here already, so I say *Hi*, and we giggle about how excited we are for Jenni and how she always used to say she would never ever get married.

I look around the room and find the table Robyn is sitting at. She is facing away from me. Her bare shoulders look soft and there are freckles on them. I can see a bobby pin in her hair.

There is a commotion near the door when the newly married couple come in. The band plays the wedding march, and Jenni sticks out her tongue towards us. Both her and Tabby are wearing a little veil on a hair clip. They hold two bouquets and throw them across the room, not backwards and coy, but front-facing, like a javelin. One lands on one of the cousins I am sitting with, who picks it up gingerly and keeps it in his lap. The other one gets caught mid-flight by one of Tabby's co-workers. Then they walk up to the top table, both grinning from ear to ear. Jenni is looking straight ahead in a daze, Tabby's eyes fixed on her. I think she might cry. Robyn is watching them too.

Much, much later, outside the hall, I queue for the taxi. Robyn stands outside too, hugging her arms to her chest against the night chill. She is talking to someone else, but hovering near me, and I know she has a room at the hotel so she isn't here waiting for a taxi.

Finally, in a vacuum of chatter, she turns to me and says, 'We didn't get a chance to talk all night!' in a tone that is all cream and strawberries. It's the way our mothers used to speak to each other when we were little. I smile and touch my finger to my mouth. I worry my lipstick has bled.

'Are you heading back into town or sticking around?' she says, because I still haven't answered. I look up at the wall of the hotel, where a few of the windows are illuminated.

'Just grabbing a taxi, yeah,' I say. I want to kick myself.

'Ah, right.' She is still lingering. I can see she wants to talk, but I don't know what about. Suddenly I worry I might cry.

'So, did you have a nice wedding?' I ask.

'I'd say. One of my favourites.'

'Yeah, it was really good, as weddings go!' I feel self-conscious saying that, as though I was asking her to marry me; I also worry Jenni is nearby and will overhear, although the last I saw of her, she was playing the grand piano in the lobby with her dress bunched up around her knees.

There is a silence and I fiddle with my phone.

'I like your hair,' I say. It looks soft.

'I like *your* hair.'

'Hey, it's not a competition,' I say.

She looks at me like a door has closed behind her eyes, but she blinks and then the expression is gone. 'So, how have you been?'

'Pretty good, you know. Can't complain.'

I want her to tell me what she's been up to so I can make a face like I don't already know, even though I've been watching along, on and off, on Facebook. She has a child. The child is two years old. She shows me a picture on her phone.

I don't know what to tell her about my life. There is too much.

I start talking about an event I hosted a few weeks ago and I realise that every single person there is someone who has come into my life after Robyn and I broke up. Everything that matters in my life has crystallised afterwards. It felt like I was suddenly free to be someone without her, I remember.

My taxi arrives, and she says goodbye. We hug, and, probably due to the copious amounts of wine I've had, I say that we should catch up properly sometime. I know that everything speaks against this, but I can't take it back. She agrees, but I can't read her eyes. She takes my phone and puts her number in it. When she hands it back to me, our fingers touch briefly; the sequins on her dress reflect in the darkness of the screen.

Freddie Alexander

CHEIROTONIA AT NEWHAVEN

Some boys sit on the dock
to hang their feet over
the lips of the sea, breath
worming out of their chest
to dust foam from the waves.

You've been holding that breath
as if air will save you. Air is just air,
held in pressure by gravity and
the weight of presence. Let it go.
Give the world all it has given you.

Some boys are sunlight on
the leaves, sensitive to changes
in temperament as gathering dew:
There is nothing wrong with you, just
stretch towards that warm light.

Love is just love. And you, good thing,
have learned love in spite of yourself.
Some boys spend their whole lives
fighting the wind in ironclad ships,
and some boys are granite rock.

If you can live your entire life
and stay kind, then yes
it is worth it.

I plant seeds in my windowsill,
hope I have done enough
to help them grow, stay to
watch that reaching for the sun.

301.4157

301 Social Sciences, Sociology, Anthropology
301.41 Family Structures
301.41x Love/Sex
301.415 you can stop here
301.4151 Gay/Lesbian History 1950-1960
301.4x52 gay/lesbian history 1960-197
301.4153 g4y/l^{esbi}an HI$/xxx 19??.exe
3011111111111111111111111
11111error111111
1x1ii1i11|11
1111.1..xxxxxxxxxxxxxxxxx
is this thing on?

301.4153 NAKED
INSECURE
PARANOID
FAGGOTRY

301.415?? the dewey decimal system first listed homosexuality in 1932, under
132 mental derangements
and
159.9 abnormal psychology

301.4155 look

closer and see

these serpents

301.iv/i/v/v Know Good and Evil

301.4156 knowledge is never neutral *not you*

not nature

301.4156999… *but the law*

'your eyes will be opened' *is wrong*

Lori England

BORROWED TROUBLE

She's come to borrow Trouble and there is no point in pretending otherwise — the black paper marks it out, though it conceals the kind. She walks with purpose past wood-covered walls and people who linger next to the section on Love. Other regulars mix it up: misery chasers, thrill seekers and aspiring writers looking for vicarious peeks into the lives of others. It's strange that she can find such sweetness in the sorrow of others, the sights, the tastes, the smells. She wants their wants so completely, she becomes subsumed in them.

She visits my library once a month, like clockwork, to return what she has borrowed. She stands on the steps with the packages bundled in dense, black paper under her arm. Four items for four weeks at a time — the maximum allowed. She never returns them before their time is up, savouring the inside of each experience so she can replay it again and again, long after it sits back in its place on the library's shelves. Each month she comes in with the same request, stalking the same section of well-worn carpet.

I can see myself in her because before it was my job, I too made old friends out of the scrapes and grooves of the shelves. It's just that my poison was Love. I mooned around different aisles and came out furtively grasping my red-wrapped packages, cheeks blushing the same colour as if someone could see the kind of love I was looking for through the paper. The kind that was not allowed.

When I was younger, I used to wonder why these sorts of experiences were allowed. Glimpses into forbidden things. Now, as their custodian, I'm not sure if it's because they are simply overlooked, or if it's thought their power can be contained by the application of thick, colour-coded wrapping paper. You don't get to be a librarian without knowledge of your subject.

But if I must be without love, at least I have a job I enjoy, and a steady, quiet life.

I am here to borrow Trouble. I know the kind I want, with its forbidden overtones of whisky and cigarette smoke. I want what is not allowed, woman trouble, the kind with a girl that makes you cry for three days straight. I borrow it from biker boys who have grown weary. I let my fingers linger over past favourites, my mind lighting up with the memory of each encounter. Pausing on the spine of 'Six Days With Susan' I suppress a shiver. I keep walking. My rule is no re-runs in the same 12-month period. It stops me slipping and being swallowed by worlds where I can touch the walls.

I have my card in my hand, name printed in bold and a picture of me, flat-faced and sharp-eyed. The card opens causeways to fingers on flesh, tinkering with inner thighs, kneading the outside of velvet knickers. A portal into lives not lived. I take my time pacing the worn stretch of faded yellow carpet, reading synopsis after synopsis before picking the perfect ones. The ones that will make returning home to my shoebox apartment seem worth it after eking out long days in my cardboard cubicle, repeating the same careworn phrases over and over.

My final choice is 'On the Beach With Beatrice.' I've fingered it a few times and put it back on the shelf. It is a rare thing: a modern setting, two women, the trouble too close to what I will bring down on my head if I ever try to get what I actually want. The ones with two women tend to be dated before the purge, or in the immediate aftermath when the reprisals for anyone found to have 'homosexual tendencies' were brutal and public.

I take my picks to the same librarian as I always do. I'll walk around a little longer if she isn't at her desk. A visit never feels complete without catching a glimpse of Miss Tunna and feeling her fingers brush mine as I exchange old experiences for new. She scans the spines and slots them in the silver letterbox; moments later, they pop out the bottom, perfectly wrapped in black.

She seems oddly distracted today, has barely smiled at me since I placed my picks on her desk.

'Is that everything, Miss Wildish?'

'Yeah, thanks, Miss Tunna. See you in four weeks.'

She doesn't wish me a good day as I leave. It's so out of rhythm with our normal interactions, I find myself staring back at her small figure. She looks stricken as if someone has just stolen her secrets.

I hadn't known it was there. Not until six months ago, when I was re-cataloguing Trouble. I was checking old experiences for flaws or skip, sending some for repair. And suddenly, there it was. 'On the Beach With Beatrice' The names are changed when experiences are donated but, once it started to play, I could see myself on those doomed days when I thought I had it in my grasp. Love; not wrapped in red paper and seen from a remove, but through the filter of someone else's eyes.

Trina must have donated it. Had she done it to hurt me? Had she known that one day I would stumble across it in the stacks and have to relive the almost perfect and the suddenly terrible? Did she want to get me fired, ostracised, forced to move, as she had been? Or did she just want rid of it? When you donate an experience, you can't quite remember it the same way, it dulls the sensations. The facts are there, but not so many of the feelings, an easing of the mind.

The worst was to feel as she had felt: the hitch in her heartbeat as her fingers touched mine; the warmth of my well-kissed bottom lip; the horror when he caught us; to feel the laughter as it died in her throat, as it had died in mine. To have the pain of it cut in from both sides, squeezing an old scar into a new shape.

I could have turned it off. I should have turned it off. We're only supposed to watch at triple speed, not immerse ourselves in the experience. They say if you watch too many, you could get lost in other people's lives. I had no idea what Mrs Trickle would say if she knew I had watched an experience where I was the leading lady. Shelved in Trouble, no less. If it had come from Comfort — a quiet day in the library, featuring some shelving, rain gently thudding on the roof — I'm sure her opinion of me would stay the same. But this? The penalties are not so harsh now that the shadow of the purge has faded, but it would still turn my warm little life upside down.

I'm barely through the door when I start. I kick my shoes off and let my coat fall and the ritual begins. The machine boots up in the corner, and I tuck my feet underneath me and carefully unwrap the black package. I feel the waxy weight of the paper under my fingers and fold it carefully on my bedside table, ready to have its contents returned.

I blink my eyes open and I am her, basking in the warmth of a place I've never been. There's sand beneath my toes and a dark-haired girl laughing on a faded blue beach towel beside me. I love her and she loves me. There is a certainty to that, a warm weight — I am swimming in contentment. Soon we wind our way up stone steps to a pale blue wooden cottage where light streams in from every direction. She kisses me, her sand coated hands rough against my cheek, her plump bottom lip sucked into my mouth. My hands slide over her smooth, sun-screen coated thighs still warm from the sun. Her hand presses into the small of my back. There are days of it, though it only takes hours to experience, and I become lost in them.

I have almost forgotten that I borrowed Trouble, not Love or Bliss. There's a reason for that: when it's over, I don't want to plunge straight from joy to the grey walls of home, alone. To the existence scraped by the skin of my teeth, shuffling through day to day feeling small. To a life where I can only exist in a horrible job by squashing myself into the wrong shape. One where I am left stealing sunlight from other people's lives. I can feel what they feel, touch what they touch but only through the filter of the machine. It's not mine. I replay it in my head as if these are my memories but they're someone else's. With Trouble, at least joy is balanced with strife.

Normally with Trouble, there's a slow build-up — tension and suspicion take hold long before the moment hits — but here there are no signs. Instead, there is ease and sweetness before the explosion. The wooden door of the little cottage hits the wall with the force of a gale, blue paint flaking and flickering in the sudden harshness of the light. Her dad is red in the face, screaming. We huddle together at first; then she slips away from me, shame written on her face. I feel the stomach-churning fear as he shouts, over and over, 'I will ruin you!'

When I come round, it comes to me that I know that girl — she's older and has lost the sweetness round the edges, but I'd know those hands anywhere.

Her small, sharp face cuts its way across the room, making a beeline for me. On another day that wouldn't have seemed strange, she always sought me out, but ever since I scanned the experience in, I have been waiting.

'Miss Wildish, good to see you again.'

It isn't, although I can't help but remember how I used to look forward to her visits, timed like clockwork, and the sight of her wending her way to my desk each time. The way she would wait if I had wandered away from my desk. I've been preparing for this but it stings all the same. I try to hide the quiver in my voice by turning up the volume on my most professional smile.

'Twice in two days — what a surprise! Is there something wrong with your experiences?'

'Nothing wrong, no.' She fumbles with the top button on her rain-slicked coat. 'I've been wondering, how is it you — how did you? I mean, what do you do to get to do a job like this? Er, I mean, how I would get started if I wanted to take it up? Could I maybe, someday, buy you coffee and you could give me advice? I mean, if it's not too much trouble.' She stumbles over words, nervous as anything.

'I'm not sure if I'm the best person to ask.'

'It doesn't have to be right away. I mean, I understand if you're too busy.'

'I'm not sure what I could tell you about getting started — I could maybe point you to the university.'

'Oh, I'm not there yet just looking for some advice on how to even start looking.'

'I could set up an appointment with Mrs Trickle, maybe?'

'I would feel so much more comfortable asking you. Right now anyway.'

She isn't going to go away, just stand there forever dripping on the carpet, looking at me with those sharp eyes. I can't tell if she's genuine or if she knows for sure. And even then what does she want — to expose me? Leverage as a way into a job, maybe? Whatever it is I need to know.

'Of course, I'd love to help another experience enthusiast get started, I used to be a lot like you. Is eight too late? That's when I finish tonight.' I am being too bright now, smiling too much. Pushing at the fear with the corners of my mouth.

'No, I'm on shift until then anyway. I'd best get back. Will I get you on the steps?'

'How about just at Charlotte's, on Old Street?'

'I know it, I'll see you there.'

Later, there she sits, two coffees in front of her, each black and unadorned. That's when I'm sure she knows. The metal seat sticks as I pull it out and sit down and, now, now that I am absolutely certain she knows about me, I steel myself for what she has to say.

'Miss Tunna,' her sharp face breaks into a wry smile, 'I'm so glad you came. I wonder, is there any way to become an experience librarian without going to university? I would love to do what you do, but I couldn't afford the fees.'

'Barely anyone can these days. I was lucky. More than lucky. My dad.' My voice cracks as I realise that she has seen my dad, red-faced and cruel, spitting hate. 'My dad paid the fees. You could do it the assistant way, I'd put in a word for you. You understand experiences in a way most people don't — very few borrow as much as you.'

'I would love that. So much. Thanks, Miss Tunna.' Her face lights up as if she has swallowed the sun, then momentarily clouds. 'I have to confess, though, I brought you here on false pretences.' She seems reluctant now and I guess she wishes she just came here for job advice because she wanted what I had offered. It feels weird to be playing this cat and mouse game, but there is no room to reveal more of ourselves than is necessary.

'Beatrice on the Beach — you are Beatrice, aren't you?'

'Yes.' I fail to keep the edge of fear from creeping into my voice this time. There is no smiling it away. 'What do you intend to do about it?'

'Nothing, no I didn't want to — ' She seems so genuinely shocked. 'And I just have... I've never met anyone like... well, me. I knew that they existed, because it was forbidden, and then because of the experiences, but never another person that I see in my day-to-day life.'

'I'm not like that anymore...' Even I can hear the false note in my voice.

'That's a shame, because I would like to kiss you. I've wanted to since the first time I saw you.' She barely whispers it, but I can feel my face flame up and I dart my eyes around to see if anyone in the surrounding area has caught the words.

'Do you have somewhere we can go?'

We leave the coffees half drunk, our eyes shining, cheeks pink, knees bumping awkwardly on the tram, sending electric charges of anticipation through me so that even my arm hairs tingle with want. The waiting weighed heavy, a fuzzy clutch in my gut. And then we are there, climbing too many stairs and only just waiting until the door swings shut until our lips meet and it all melts into the background and becomes the muffled noise outside a closed window. There is only the taste of her tongue, the feel of her skin under my fingertips as I push her shirt up and over her head, and the hammering of my heart in my ears.

Soon I'll start working at the customer service desk. Mrs Trickle said there was no-one better, and they'll have me cataloguing in no time. Until then I visit the library once a week, pink-cheeked to return what I have borrowed. Maybe a trip halfway around the world, or a journey into space. I have a bigger place closer to the city, and a roommate who's really my lover. We watch together, me and Miss Tunna, only occasionally immersing ourselves entirely. I feel her skin under my fingertips, kiss her with my own lips, feel the fragile love she has cast over me like a protective spell.

I don't need to borrow Trouble any more. I just need it to stay away from our door.

Bibi June

LEGACY

Do you remember
the first time you held pronouns
in your mouth like sacrament?

Do you forget
the first brick thrown,
the first kiss after the vote.

Forget to go to church,
forget that theirs were
carved from empty hearses.

That DNA does not answer
all questions, like how
do we honour our ancestors

when blood is the least of our
likeness, blood is the street
and the fight that happens on it.

It is the gritty reality of our history,
the past of our found family,
whose prayers we answer.

Do not be callous with your
newfound rapture.
This is only another chapter.

Do you remember?
The first time you wrote
your name into the scriptures.

Did you flick back
through the pages
before staking claim?

Do not mistake this for gatekeeping.
There is something divine
about your carefree enjoyment.

Where the wine flows from
tongue to lips to lips to
making love for the first time.

Eagerly, like learning how to swim.
Fear slowly swallowed
by muscle memory.

This normalcy is hard-fought.
Do not be complicit in its erasure
If not by way of remembrance, then

by building altars for the bodies
you embrace. Worshipping the people
you surround yourself with.

Make a pantheon out of your friends.
This was never just about romance,
it was about love and finding god

in the curve of her back, his lips
their kiss. In that moment of ecstasy,
head between your hips.

Moaning- oh god, oh god,
like so many before you
have called out in prayer.

Jo Clifford

THESE ARE MY HANDS

These are my hands
My dad paid for me to have carpentry lessons
Because he thought it would be good for me to make things out of wood
But I couldn't do that
These hands cannot make things
My dad paid for me to have boxing lessons
Because he thought it would be good for me to learn how to fight
But I couldn't do that
These hands were not made to hit people.
So instead I burst into tears.
These are my feet
My dad paid for them to be encased in army boots
Which I was supposed to spit and polish
And march up and down in army uniform
Learn to clean a rifle, point it at a target,
And shoot to kill.
But I couldn't do that.
These feet were not made for marching.
In here is my brain
My dad wanted me to use it to become a business man
Or perhaps a diplomat.
But I couldn't do that.
This brain was not made to exploit or lie.

My poor dad.
I really was not the person that he wanted me to be at all.
So who was I?
This is my face.
For many years it was a man's face and when I looked in the mirror
I could never believe that it was mine
But then these hands
These hands learnt to hold my children
These hands learnt to comfort them when they were hurt or were afraid
These hands learnt to caress my lover
And give them joy and pleasure.
These hands learnt to communicate my love.
With these hands I learnt to write
With these hands I've written almost ninety plays.
So many words. About a million.
About a million words.
No wonder my hands hurt sometimes.
With these legs I was supposed to run fast and defeat my opponents in football, or in cricket, or in rugby games.
With these legs I was supposed to march like a soldier
And walk like a man erect and strong.
These legs are damaged because for many years
I tried to walk a path that was not my own.
My heart is damaged too. Hurt by shame.
Broken by grief and bitter loss.
My heart is held together by plastic ring
Placed inside a valve to stop it bleeding.
I can only walk because they replaced my hip and knee
I carry the scars
Here. Here. And here.
They are like wounds that I received in battle
The long relentless battle to become my self.
The battle we all must fight some day.

The lines on my face tell of the progress of the fight
Its defeats and victories.
But now when I look in the mirror I don't see a stranger boy or man
I see myself.
I may not like what I see
The baggy eyes, double chin, thinning hair
All the signs of my ageing.
But I know they're mine.
And when I look in the mirror I wish myself well
Wish myself well on this lifelong journey
The journey I am making towards my own dear self.
One day this heart will be worn out
On that day it will stop beating
And then I'll know.
Then I'll know my destination.

Edinburgh, 20th October 2016.

Elaine Gallagher

OUTSIDE, IT'S ALWAYS SUMMER

She dreams. Their flat is airy, bright; white walls sunlit by tall windows, decorated with small seascapes in peaceful blues and greens. The tree-lined boulevard outside is dappled with shade from fresh spring leaves, newly burst from buds, and carpeted with apple and cherry blossom.

She and her love spend leisurely hours watching the easy bustle of the street below, sharing kisses and pastries and crisp white wine, young women enchanted with each other's promise. Half-dressed, she poses for Lotte to paint, in her head composing songs. In the evening they walk arm in arm to the square by the cathedral, to cafes lit by lanterns of coloured glass, to tables under awnings by the square where her love is feted by artists and envied for her talent and the beauty of her subject.

They dine lightly and move on to the clubs and the musicians and the night life. She sings — new songs of passion to the one woman in the audience who matters to her, and old songs from the old country, of war and loss, of fighting and defeat, of retreat and exile and preserving all that might be saved, traditions and stories and identity.

Josef wakes. Heats water for tea and to wash, on a little gas ring in a corner of his room by the grimy window. Bare floor boards creak as he washes, dresses. The iron bedstead groans as he sits to drink. He throws the lees of his tea out the window into the filthy alley, then puts on shirt and collar, jacket and tie, picks up his hat and overcoat, and goes to work.

He does what he's told, and keeps his head down. Every day in the bureau he checks memos for policy, reads stock reports and warehouse tallies, writes requisitions to suppliers, reports to superiors. The managerial mechanism is as caring of its components as any other machine and he leaves the office every day a little more worn down.

The songs of his dream thunder in his mind through the day.

She dreams and she paints. Her love, Serafina, poses for her nude, or in gauzy dresses, or dances around their apartment, sunlit. They kiss on the couch, explore each other's bodies with trails of kisses, trailing fingers; fall into bed laughing, caressing, fucking. They share languid conversations in the afterglow; what it is to be women, what it is to be free, what it is to be in love.

They pass the afternoons on the balcony, she in dungarees, Sera in a gown. Surrounded by trees, enough above the boulevard that no-one can catch the glimpses of their bodies that each gives to the other, and to no-one else. In evenings and evening dress they dine in the city, she dashing in white tie and tails, hair short beneath her top hat, Sera elegant on her arm. They meet artists and poets in the square of lights; Sera sings revolutionary songs in little clubs, and after, they dance.

Charlotte gets the weans up and dressed and has breakfast on the table for himself. When they're out, she packs the sheets in her trolley and lugs them over to the laundry. The girls there will have them spotless. The sisters will see to it. On her way home she gets the messages, chops for his tea. He'll be back from the yard at five o'clock and hungry.

It's a good life. She's a good wife and he's a good husband. He brings his pay packet home to her unbroken on a Friday, and he doesn't hit her. She gives him his money for beer, and his pieces for his lunch, and she gets the weans to mass on a Sunday, and the old women don't talk about her. They stay out of politics and the politics leaves them alone.

Now and then they talk about moving, going to America, to the big cities that they see in the pictures, but they're doing alright where they are. He has his work and she has her house. At the Fair, they take the weans to the country, spend a week at her cousins' farm. She relaxes in the fresh air, away from the Belfast smoke. He helps dig peat for the fire and she draws the hills and the lough in her sketch book.

It's best that way. If she had come to the attention of the old women or the priests, she could have ended up another fallen woman in the laundry under the sisters' thumb, working her sins out of her. She was a good girl and found a good man. Sometimes she draws from her dreams; nudes of a beautiful woman, someone cool and slightly cruel. She tears out those pages and lights the fire with them.

Josef finds songs running through his head, distracting him; words of another country he has never known, songs of sorrow and exile. He puts them out of his mind during the day — they are fantasies; romance. He was born in a village outside Prague and this is his country right where he is, although ruled now from Moscow, and before from Berlin, and before then from Vienna. In the evenings he takes his meal in a cafe at the end of the Bridge of Kings, and amid the music and dancing he writes his songs down.

The city of Josef's dream is not a place he has ever seen in waking. As Sera, she walks in bright gardens and eats in graceful auberges, enjoys a freedom of art and music and debate which he would not find in Prague in this time. But time passes and Prague becomes more like the dream; Bohemian poets and playwrights raise their voices in criticism of the dour Soviet ideologies, mock them with jokes that they can't understand or abide.

Josef raises his voice with them, singing songs that he

remembers from the dream, of an old country that has never existed. When the tanks roll and the fist closes again, the censors declare that he is decadent and corrupt. His songs are veiled protest, they say; criticism of the regime. Fantasy is not permitted.

He will be silent in prison.

While Josef sleeps in a cell, Sera sings, and poses for Lotte to paint. In dreams they travel. Sera takes Lotte to painted dachas in forested Alps, where they warm each other by wood fires. Outside, the wind and other things howl and demand entry with threats. Inside, they embrace on fur rugs, each safe in the other's arms, and shut out the clamour. They talk of freedom; what lives they might lead, if only they dared.

Lotte dares. She takes Sera to glittering cities, where cars rush along streets between towers of glass. In a sunlit park she plaits flowers in Sera's hair; they listen to beat poets in coffee bars. They have adventures and run hand in hand along mean streets, one step ahead of the Man.

In Belfast, Catholic and Protestant, Republican and Unionist, snarl at each other. Fathers pass hatred down to sons in fighting and marching, and mothers keep their silence, or walk along. Each side is as puritan as the other, the paramilitaries as quick to punish moral failings as they are to root out traitors.

With the Troubles, and the bombs, and the army on every corner, Charlotte dreams of a city of beautiful women and dances with her Sera, free of the rule of men with fists and guns. She is careful to burn her sketches, and never look too long at another woman.

Josef stands, blinking in the spring morning outside the prison gate. He has stepped only into a more spacious confinement. The Soviets are still in command through their puppet governors, and the people they have released so far are unemployable;

silenced by fear and poverty. There is nothing for him here, but in his head he has a dream of a city of glass, with yellow cars on thronged tarmac streets. He starts walking.

Charlotte can't do it any more. Her husband never lifts a hand to her, no; but they have hard words and he ends up sleeping on the sofa. More and more often, she starts the fight so that she doesn't have to share her bed with him. He tries to accuse her, that there's another man, but there never has been. When he says this the women silence him; even the parish priest supports her. In the eyes of the Church after all, celibacy is not a sin, especially after four children.

Josef has nothing but the clothes he is standing in. He finds old friends, a floor to sleep on, a few crowns for his pocket. In his dreams, Sera and Lotte live in a loft together in a bustling city of ironwork and brown stone. They wear denim and bright colours, drink beer on the building roof, gaze across foothills of tenement buildings to the glass and steel spires on the horizon. He makes his way to Prague, to the palace where the Americans have their embassy. No-one pays attention to a shabby Czech, walking through the gardens to ask for asylum.

The weans are all grown and have jobs. It's the seventies, and her daughters don't have to depend on finding a man to keep them. Charlotte takes her savings and takes the boat, to her cousins in New York, to the skyscrapers and the yellow cabs that she's seen in the pictures. Maybe she won't have to be so careful there.

Charlotte paints in a loft in Greenwich village. She doesn't tell her cousins that she has met someone, a woman whose face fascinated her when she was sketching street scenes. For all their Irish-American ebullience, her extended family still keep a lot of the old country in their souls. Her new love moves in with her a few months later.

Josef plays guitar and violin in basement bars; folk music is popular and he makes a good living, writing and recording popular songs. Every now and then he makes a statement or a recording for the authorities, how this is a land of opportunity and he is grateful to be here. Each year he watches the marchers go past; all the gay people celebrating the anniversary of a riot that happened while he was in prison. He doesn't join them; it's not for him. But he smiles at the thought that they can march like that without meeting tanks. Perhaps, back home, that will be true one day.

Josef dreams. Charlotte dreams. Sera meets Lotte in a cafe on Bleecker Street, far from where they started. They smile, chat, drink coffee, hold hands. Lotte looks up; another woman is approaching, and she waves. She goes to the woman, and they kiss.

On a balcony above a boulevard, Sera watches two women kiss. She picks up her violin and begins to play.

BD Owens

FATHERS, DO NOT EXASPERATE YOUR CHILDREN

EPHESIANS 6:4

I was
a defiant youth
but lucky
because he never beat me.
Instead
he used punishing words
Bible quotations
woven with malice
and guilt brocade.

Until then
I had never seen him so angry.
Puce
a hot dark purple
the colour of his face and neck
when suppressing rage.

It was just one line of text.
New Testament scripture
my perfect ammunition
slipped right in
with no come back.

It just fell into place.
Luck?
A gift?
His line
then mine
but mine
continued the verse.

TORNADOS SWEEP BALLAT CROSS

Our ancient whinstone
farmhouse shuddered
under a practice
warpath.

Low flying
fighter jets
scorched the
treetops.

A second's pause

brought a deafening wail
launching our geese
scrambling for height
breaching the
stock fence boundary.
Just enough lift
to traverse the valley.
Fragments of white
wing tips strewn
in their wake.

After searching
we would find them
huddled under hedges.
A flimsy comfort.

One by one

I gathered them
to my breast.
Their warm tense
feathery bodies
pulsing heartbeats
against my ribs.
Long sleek necks
wrapped around mine.

Ross Jamieson

CIRCLES

Jasper, 2018

In a freshly tarmacked lay-by a plinth, carved from the same scaled grey stone that punctures the landscape, bears a plaque that gives the bridge's history. It was built in the fifties — before that a ferry carried people back and forth across the sea loch. A poorly scanned old photograph reproduced on the plaque shows a man in a suit and a woman in a white dress sitting in a precarious-looking wooden dinghy. Their faces are a reprographic blur, white and grey pixels under blocky black shocks of hair. It's not clear if they are coming to the small island or leaving. Jasper lifts his camera and snaps a picture, a further degradation.

The sky is overcast, but the sun is bright behind the clouds — the white paint on the bridge gleams, a needle to the back of his tired eyes. He took the early ferry to save on a night's accommodation. Jasper starts up the slope behind and sees the stones silhouetted atop the bluff overlooking the bridge. The tall shapes seem to blur and shift, until his eyes focus and he sees the children, darting like foxes between the stones in some senseless game. They freeze when they spy Jasper and, after a glance at one another and a burst of laughter, peel off into the hills. When he reaches the crest of the hill and looks out they are nowhere to be seen, though a smatter of high voices reaches him, broken on the wind.

With his gaze in the distance, Jasper inadvertently kicks something with his foot and sends it skittering across the grass. A clutch of pebbles lie at his feet, all smooth, round and bright — all chosen. They have been arranged in a formation, but he has spoiled it by walking into it and can't tell what it was supposed to be. He raises his camera, snaps another picture, then sets to work in earnest.

The group is incomplete — four great slabs in a semi-circle concave to the water, erratically spaced like a mouth of broken teeth. Not an unkind mouth, though. Jasper starts taking pictures and making sketches in a drawing pad, of the stones' layout and their alignments. Three of the menhirs stand in a row, with a fourth off on its own, right by the cliff edge, almost leaning over the sagging wire fence. The scattering of pebbles left by the children lay in the spot where a fifth stone might have stood. Thoughts, ideas start to come, unexpected pathways forming between the stones, the sea, the hazy outline of the horizon.

His stone prints began selling last year after he posted the first of them online. It was originally intended as a one-off, inspired by a visit to the Twelve Apostles in Dumfries, but it quickly sold out, giving Jasper his first taste of success. He began visiting stone circles up and down the country, combining elements of the stones and the landscape with diagrammatic line drawings based on the circles' ancient geometry. He gives them titles plucked from the self-help section of bookshops: *Mindfulness for Everyday Living*; *How to Change Your Life in 15 Minutes a Day*; *How to Stop Binge-Eating*. The owner of the gallery where Jasper sells the most prints said they were the perfect balance of irony and vague, pastoral reassurance.

The stone by the cliff is shorter than the others, hunched almost, with some kind of bushy lichen spreading over its shoulders like a shawl. She's waiting for someone, Jasper thinks, the thought breaking unbidden, like air escaping a seal. Her grey face is turned towards the bridge as though she expects someone to cross it, though she's been standing far longer than the bridge has. He notices the fronded grass covering a field on the other side of the channel — the leaves have a silvery underbelly that flicks up in the wind, aping the chop of the water below. The curve of the semi-circle seems to focus on that spot like a lens. Jasper wonders if something might have stood there once, some structure. Some significant thing.

A familiar ping sounds from his jacket pocket. Jasper takes out his phone, surprised that he has a signal. Way in the distance the stark lines of a telecom tower break the horizon, a faint red light blinking intermittently. He opens the app, his thumb finding the accustomed spot: a lot of blank squares here, faceless outlines without names. One of them has sent him a message. Jasper usually ignores the ones without faces. He puts the phone away and takes up his sketch pad again.

He descends the slope and crosses the bridge on foot. Climbing the fence on the other side he walks out into the field of silvering grass. He doesn't find anything, of course, but he likes to let his imagination wander over the possibilities. His phone pings again, another message, this time a picture. He ignores it, but finds himself scrolling over the profiles again, as if they might be different on this side of the bridge. Easier just to imagine the possibilities. The grass flicks around him, mercurial.

When he returns to the stone circle a little dog is ferreting around in the gorse bushes nearby. A wee thing, skull the size of a fist with eyes bulging out like golf balls. It yaps and starts up a skittish dance at Jasper's feet, eventually calming down and allowing itself to be scratched behind the ear. The dog's owner is preceded by the stiff crackle of her waterproof. She smiles at him and calls the dog — Jasper doesn't catch its name. The wind seems to carry words away with it.

'You'll be the kidnapper, then,' she calls to Jasper, in the tone of a friendly greeting.

'Excuse me?' He freezes momentarily, until she laughs.

'I passed the kids on the way,' she says. 'They said they were running from a kidnapper. Just ignore them if they bother you, they run absolutely wild in the holidays.'

'Ah, I see,' Jasper says. 'I think I interrupted their game.' He gestures at the pebbles on the ground.

'Oh, do they still do that? How funny. Girls have been doing that since my time.' She sits down on a flat stone ledge and takes a packet of cigarettes from her pocket. Jasper declines her offer of one, so she lights up herself and carries on, scratching her head through her short, steely hair. 'We used to call that the magic spot, where they've got the pebbles there. They used to say that if you stood there and faced in just the right direction you would see the man you were going to marry standing in the field opposite there.'

'The one with the long grass?'

'That's it. All nonsense, of course, just tea leaves and apple stalks.'

'Did you ever try it?'

'Of course, and if you ask me now I'll tell you I saw my own husband in the field and that'll be my final answer.' She laughs to herself. 'But, do you know, it's been that long I don't think I could tell you who I saw, or who I wanted to see. Might as well just make it the one I ended up with, eh? For neatness' sake.'

'The past is what you make of it, I suppose.'

She is quiet then and for a moment seems to be looking at something else, something not there in front of either of them. 'Sorry,' she shakes herself. 'Deja vu. When I was young, an archaeologist came here to look at the stones. You made me think of that, just now. How funny. It must be forty years since it's even occurred to me.' She spies his camera, his sketch pad. 'Is that the kind of thing you're doing?'

Jasper tells her he is an artist, explains the series he is working on. She makes him write his social media accounts down on a sheet from his pad and tells him she'll find him on her tablet when she gets home. The little dog darts ahead of her when she moves to go, yapping at insects or mice in the bushes, or possibly nothing. Jasper watches until they're out of sight, then turns to go back to his rental car. He pauses by the circle of pebbles for a moment, then scatters them all with his foot and heads down the slope.

They meet for a drink in the bar in Jasper's hotel. They chat. The guy is nice, if underneath it all essentially disinterested. Jasper knows he must come across the same way, like some essential part of himself has retreated into a corner and won't come out no matter how it's coaxed. He's done it a lot this last year, these hookups. It's easy, when you're on the road, to take your face off and become a blank for the night.

They go upstairs and the whole evening is done and showered off in about two hours. They have no past, no future, only a present together, two points in time folded together so that the intervening moments seem to vanish.

Stanley, 1965

The way the road insinuates itself around the hills makes him queasy, so he keeps his face in the stream of cold air from the window. Chris, his driver for the day, steers almost as if by memory. Stanley watches his practiced turns of the wheel until he feels nauseous again and returns to the window, though his thoughts remain with the thick black hair on Chris's forearms that extends like a creeping vine onto the backs of his hands.

Stanley heard him called by some nickname in the lounge last night, but wasn't sure he had heard it correctly and didn't want to try it for fear of mispronouncing it. He was reading the paper at a corner booth, the rest of the group from the university having retired to bed; the group of locals at the bar all filed out eventually, except for Chris, who wandered over to Stanley's table, swirling the dregs of his pint in his glass as if he'd kept them back just for that purpose.

He asked if Stanley was with the archaeologists. Stanley said he was. He asked what sites they had visited and Stanley told him. He asked if he was interested in seeing another stone circle. Stanley said he was. All the while Chris swirled the meagre remains of his pint, looking down at them occasionally whenever he felt they had held eye contact a bit too long.

As he expected, the rest of the group had not been interested in visiting another site, particularly such an outlying one. They rarely credited anything Stanley told them and besides, they were going fishing. They didn't like him and didn't ask themselves why — there is an uncanny instinct that people possess, Stanley has found, for identifying difference in a person without having to articulate it. The moment they met they sorted him into a pile like a chicken sexer. But the stone circle on the island might be worth seeing, Stanley told himself. It might be worth a shot.

Really, though, it's something else whispering in his ear that has put him in a van being driven by complete stranger to the far side of a wild and sparse island. Something soft as silk and possessed of the surprising strength of that fabric as well — F it pulls him, gently, firmly, could pull him further, he knows, beyond prudence, beyond all care, even. Just a whisper and yet it fills his sails like a powerful wind.

Stanley gets out of the van just past the bridge. Chris will pick him up again once he's delivered the post.

'I'll be about half-an-hour. But if you need longer,' he is quick to add, 'I can wait. I'm in no hurry.'

'Thank you, I really appreciate this.' The conversation passes like an unfinished sneeze. Something lies between them that they can't quite grasp, as if the limb they would use to do it has atrophied from disuse. Chris drives off and Stanley climbs the slope up to where the stone circle sits perched above the water.

And a little thing it is, too, when compared with the grand geometry of the sites they have visited prior. They are a rather forlorn group, one in particular hunched as if against the cold, or in mourning for the apparent loss of one of their number. The wind is sharp, indeed, running cold fingers through Stanley's hair, riling the sea and seeming to stir his thoughts as well. Generally he prefers the safe prospect of stagnation and a well-sealed room. The wind cuts through as if he had no walls at all. He takes a notebook from his satchel and begins measuring, recoding, sketching.

Looking up the hill he sees a girl walking towards him, face soft in easy thoughts. She hasn't noticed him and stops short when she does, making Stanley feel guilty for spying on her unguarded moment. Her hand is frozen in the process of pulling something from the pocket of her coarse-looking cardigan. She frowns and leaves the object where it is, approaching Stanley instead. She doesn't introduce herself, but asks what he's doing. While he explains, she listens, but seems to still be irked by something. She keeps looking back the way she came.

'Expecting someone?' Stanley asks, worried he might have intruded upon some teenage tryst. The girl's eyes widen in surprise for a moment.

'Not really,' she says. 'It's just that my wee sister likes to follow me.'

'And you don't want her telling your mother you've been out smoking again?' Stanley smiles and raises an inquisitive eyebrow. The girl gives him a sharp look, then follows his gaze down to where the cigarette packet is sticking out of her cardigan pocket. She flusters for a second.

'She's such a wee rat, she'd walk to town with no shoes just to tell my mother I farted.' Stanley laughs and the girl seems pleased, briefly, that a grown man would laugh at anything she said.

'Go on and smoke if you want to,' he says. 'I won't tell.' He produces his own cigarettes from his jacket pocket and offers her one. They puff away quietly for a bit, Stanley finishing up his observations, the girl wandering among the stones.

'They call this the magic spot, you know,' she says, placing her feet together on the spot where Stanley thought another menhir might once have stood.

'Oh yes?'

'They say that if you stand here and look over there in that field you'll see the man you're going to marry.'

'Who says?'

'Well, I don't know. Old folk. Wee girls.'

'They can tell the future can they, the stones?' Stanley asks. 'Well dash it all, here I was hoping they would tell me something about the past.'

'Wouldn't it be better to know about the future than the past, though?' She asks, a note of sincerity rising through the play.

'I don't know about that,' he says. 'What if we don't like what we see?' She considers this for a moment and Stanley worries he has caused some real disappointment. She rallies, however.

'Anyway, its just a feeling you get. A game.' She puts out her cigarette on one of the stones and flicks the butt over the cliff edge. 'I need to get back. Enjoy the past.' At that she strides off, cardigan tails whipping, seemingly impervious to the cold, and is soon out of sight.

Stanley finds the spot where the girl stood and looks over the water, wondering which field she meant. One fenced off square catches his eye, flashing green and silver in the wind. The sound of an engine draws his attention and Chris' van round the corner towards the bridge. He slips a little coming down the slope to the road.

Better to stick to the past, he thinks. Looking ahead, the future always seems so precipitous, an uncontrollable downward slide.

Chris turns the van off the main road and onto a flattened dirt track. They pull into a small quarry, out of use, out of sight. The engine cuts and rattles, the van stills. They don't look at one another. They might never. It's amazing the things you can do with a person and never look at them, in the back of a van, in some tangled corner of woodland, at the bottom of a steep slope.

Only this time they do look, Stanley and Chris. For all that it's hard to meet the other's eye and see everything it reflects, they look. For all that the other man's gaze seems to tell their futures plain as day, they look.

Jasper, 2018

The day's sailings have been cancelled due to the weather. Jasper, unsure what to do with himself, is drawn back to the little stone circle. The wind hits him like a thousand pushing hands, it drags white spray across the surface of the water in long streaks like scratch marks on a wall. Jasper climbs the slope and sits on the flat stone ledge, continually nudged by the wind. He looks idly in case the old woman appears again, but given the weather it seems unlikely. He gets up.

It's not hard to find the spot again, even without the pebbles to mark it. He steadies himself against the wind, looks down at his feet, the toes of his boots wet from the grass. Looks up at the violently shaking grass, silver, green, silver, green.

MJ Brocklebank

EXCERPT FROM: BECOMING DOCTOR BARRY

SCENE FOUR

Barry's cottage, Cape Town, 1819.

Barry LIMPS in, clutching his right thigh, which has a bandage below his ripped breeches. He is agitated, energised — and in pain. Georgina hurries in after him, distressed.

GEORGINA
You're hurt!

BARRY
It's nothing, a scratch. Please Georgie, go back to the house.

Barry locates his medical bag and begins to rifle through it.

GEORGINA
Sit down and let me look at your wound. Oh James, how could you do this?

BARRY
I'll attend to myself... I am the physician after all.

GEORGINA
You're a wicked man! You could have got yourself killed.

BARRY

I very much doubt that. Cloete was never going to get the better of me. Damn upstart.

GEORGINA

He is a soldier, you are a doctor — as you so often like to point out.

BARRY

And a very fine one at that. So, if you would be so kind as to leave me alone then I will administer to myself.

GEORGINA

Take off those breeches at once. Let me help you…

She goes to help remove his breeches.

BARRY

Most certainly not. Now, let me do this.

Barry sits, turns away from Georgina. He rips the breeches further up his thigh and begins to attempt to change the bandage. Georgina watches from a little way behind him.

GEORGINA

You are an insufferable man, James Barry. But you're fully aware of that fact, aren't you?

BARRY

My patients don't happen to think so.

GEORGINA

That's because the only people you are kind to are your patients. The rest of us have to endure your more unpleasant disposition.

BARRY

I'm not kind to you?

GEORGINA

No… sometimes… yes, on occasion, yes you are kind to me.

BARRY

I thought we were friends, Georgina?

GEORGINA

I'd say that it was quite presumptuous of you to think that you, Doctor, could be friends with the Governor's daughter.

BARRY

Oh do forgive me, Miss Somerset, I spoke out of turn.

GEORGINA

As you often do, Doctor Barry. (*Indicating his wound*) And there, there is the consequence of that tongue of yours. And what of Cloete?

BARRY

What of the scoundrel?

GEORGINA

Is he injured?

Barry finishes tying the new bandage and turns back to Georgina.

BARRY

I'm afraid not.

GEORGINA

Thank the heavens.

BARRY

(He mimes putting a pistol to his forehead)

I got him right there. Bang!

GEORGINA

Oh James no, no!

BARRY

It's true. *(Beat)* Unfortunately, the peak of his cap checked the blow and he's perfectly fine, not a scratch on his young Dutch head.

GEORGINA

(After a beat of disbelief) How could you? How could you let me think that you had killed the poor man?

BARRY

Poor man? He pulled my nose!

GEORGINA

Because you insulted my father.

BARRY

No, no I won't have it. I would never insult your father and you know that to be true.

GEORGINA

Then what was it you said that so drove Captain Cloete to demand a duel?

BARRY

It was I that demanded the duel. I will not have my nose pulled by anyone, let alone a snivelling toady like Cloete.

GEORGINA

So that was it? Jealousy for my father's attention?

BARRY

Certainly not.

GEORGINA

You know how dear he holds you, don't you? We both do. You cannot pretend you're not aware of that?

BARRY

And he is dear to me. I'm grateful for everything he has done for me, I promise you.

GEORGINA

Then why do you constantly test him like you do? He has his limits.

A pause.

BARRY

Where is Lord Somerset? Is he aware of what transpired this morning?

GEORGINA

(She nods) He had some business to deal with.

BARRY

He's always had some business to deal with, ever since I have known him.

GEORGINA

I think… I think on this occasion it may not have been regarding the running of the Colony. I think it could be about marriage. (*Off his surprised look*) My marriage.

BARRY

Your marriage?

GEORGINA

Is that such a surprise to you? That I might have suitors?

BARRY

No, no… well, perhaps it is of some small surprise.

GEORGINA

And at my age…

BARRY

But your father needs you. He relies on you entirely when it comes to household matters.

GEORGINA

I'm afraid that would no longer be possible if I went to England to marry, would it?

BARRY

England? I didn't realise.

GEORGINA

Unless there was something to keep me here? Someone to keep me here?

In the following pause, Georgina leans in to kiss Barry. Shocked, he pulls away from her.

BARRY

Miss Somerset!

Angry at the rejection, she doesn't know what to say.

BARRY

Georgina... I think... you know how much I think of you...

GEORGINA

But you want me to go away, is that it? All the way to England? Because that's what will happen. We'll be parted forever.

BARRY

I wouldn't want that, you must know that to be true.

GEORGINA

Then all you have to do is ask me...

BARRY

Georgie, you don't understand...

GEORGINA

I understand perfectly well. I know you both better than you think. I always have.

Silence.

BARRY

I have quite lost your meaning.

GEORGINA

Perhaps you think my father wouldn't approve of you and me?

BARRY

I certainly wouldn't dare to speculate on what he thought on many topics, but on that one, I have no doubt.

GEORGINA

Then ask me James! Ask me...

Silence.

BARRY

I cannot. If you truly know me, you know I cannot.

Crushed, Georgina turns and HURRIES to the door — and comes face-to-face with Lord Somerset in the doorway. She glares at her father, before running out. As Somerset enters, Barry gets up stiffly from the chair.

SOMERSET

You're a lucky man. *(Off Barry's silence)* Captain Cloete is still alive.

BARRY

Charles—

SOMERSET

Though it seems his shako is missing its peak. And you look in need of new britches.

BARRY

I couldn't let him get away with what he did.

SOMERSET

Unfortunately for me, it seems you never can.

BARRY

He insulted me Charles, my good name was at stake.

SOMERSET

And it will be up to me to defend it once again to the authorities at home.

Barry begins to once more search his medical bag for something to help with his pain.

SOMERSET

For heaven's sake sit down man, you're hurt. (*Barry sits*) I hear Cloete turned quite pale.

BARRY

Perhaps he wasn't expecting my aim to be so true. Well, he knows better now. And the rest of them and their blasted jibes.

SOMERSET

You are too sensitive, I've said this before.

BARRY

Please, don't call me that. Was I too sensitive when I nursed you back to life last year? When I fed you, bathed you and saw to your toilet? Was I too sensitive to see you come so close to death but stay by your side and not let you slip away from me? No, sir, I was not too sensitive to endure that.

SOMERSET

You were magnificent.

A long look between them.

SOMERSET

When I heard Cloete had shot you, I thought the worst. I thought you might be… that would be too much to b.

BARRY

It's nothing, a flesh wound.

SOMERSET

Let me see…

Somerset goes towards Barry.

BARRY

No! Please, the wound will heal. You know my skills.

SOMERSET

I do indeed. Intimately. James, if you had died—

BARRY

You would have had need to send for another doctor. He wouldn't have been quite like me but you would have forgotten me in time.

SOMERSET

No, he wound not have been quite like you.

Another look between them — longing.

SOMERSET

And imagine how Georgie would have taken it?

BARRY

Georgina would also forget me, in time. Especially with the distraction of a husband.

Beat.

SOMERSET

A husband? What do you say?

BARRY

There is really no need to pretend. You're taking her back to London to marry her off. I'm glad for her. At her age, a woman should be married. It's absolutely the right thing to do.

SOMERSET

James, I don't know what she has told you, but—

BARRY

I understand perfectly. You wouldn't want a rogue like me marrying your daughter, would you?

Silence.

SOMERSET

It is I who is to marry.

Silence. Barry is quite still.

SOMERSET

James?

BARRY

That's wonderful news, Lord Somerset, most wonderful news. When do you sail for England?

SOMERSET

Soon.

BARRY

I wish you Godspeed and a pleasant voyage. *(A pause)* When will you be back?

SOMERSET

That is yet to be decided. James—

BARRY

You are coming back, aren't you?

SOMERSET

This colony can't run itself. I'm needed here.

BARRY

You certainly are.

Silence. Somerset wants to comfort Barry. He notices Barry's wound is bleeding through the bandage.

SOMERSET

Your wound, it's bleeding—

He goes closer to Barry.

BARRY

It's nothing… it's… just a scratch.

They are close now, intimate—

Barry leans in and kisses Somerset.

After a moment, they pull apart, breathless. And then they lean in again and they kiss again. With passion. Somerset lays his hand on Barry's wound.

SOMERSET

Does it hurt?

BARRY

Yes.

Taking Somerset's hand, Barry guides it up from his wound, up his inner thigh, up and up until it is deep between Barry's legs. Startled, Somerset goes to step back — but Barry keeps him held there. They stare at each other, close.

SOMERSET

James?

BARRY

I love you.

They kiss. And then Somerset helps Barry to his feet and Barry leads Somerset off.

CALLUM HARPER

TO BE DIVINE

Wooden stages hold scars
Christened by the stilettos of wayward performers.
Tonight, this garnet bourbon night,
She burned a buxom silhouette caressing the neon grime
In some seedy bar only fit for this city's beautiful swine.
Brows pulled straight to heaven, essential for the fantasy,
touching ratty pearl.
Divine. We play in the shadows of your giant heart as the
flamingos
Cry for the decline of their filthy bloodline.
But in a moment, in this dingy hovel on Hope street, her
spirit swims in the floodlight.
From a bloodied-peacock lip bellows a tide of shock
Tinged with a lifetime of tragedy. But those bruises and
atrocities
Soothe the madness of the gutter kids, safe in the gloom,
Laughing at life, just for a second.
And in that second, she was utterly, foolishly happy.
And with the stumbling exodus of 3 AM,
She'll return upstairs to her one-room home,
Break the magic of a covered lid, the glamour of a budget
dress, and look out the window.
Rain falls past the pale lamplight
Glinting as it hits off his roughened skin. His vision drifts
into white
As dawn breaks — brighter than Broadway.

Shane Strachan

ARE YOU LONESOME TONIGHT?

To me, he seemed a delicate man at first. I'll always remember the squares of light from the disco ball sliding across his pale face. He was leaning on the bar up the back, away from the jeering crowd at my feet — another tough night. The only time they'd laughed was when I tripped over my dress as I got on stage. It was the same lot who'd heard all the punch lines before, except for him.

My time was up, thank god. I shuffled off the stage and the next act got on: Rusty Springfield. She started with a song and the crowd seemed to like that better, became placid. I snuck round the side of them and ordered a coke at the bar. I downed it as fast as I could and an ice cube slipped down my throat. I started to choke and a firm hand patted at the top of my back.

Ye okay?

It was the pale man. The ice dissolved enough for me to swallow.

Just about, I coughed. He smiled, and ran his fingers through the hair across my shoulders.

Would ye like another drink? Maybe something a bittie stronger? Magnified by his large glasses, his eyes looked kind, or maybe just pitiful.

Sure.

That's how it started. He kept buying us rum and cokes and

we told each other about our lives.

I didn't have much to say. I was just a student and not much else was going on around that time. But it was enough for him to tell me about his childhood in Scotland, his years as a cook in the army, and his life in London so far. The more he spoke, the more I was intrigued. He wasn't the nicest to look at, but his floppy brown hair and glasses soon became endearing in a nerdy way. I played with his hair and, even though he was much older than me, joked that I wanted to mother him.

After an hour or so of chatting, he showed me that his wallet was empty. No more drinks. I got up off my bar stool, kissed him on the cheek and walked away.

John, he called out after me. Come back to mine. We can hae a drink there.

Finally! I said. I thought you'd never ask. I'm dying to get out this place.

Wig, dress and make up off, I met him out the front of the club. I was worried he wouldn't like me as a man. Some of them were like that, but he smiled when he saw me, said he knew it was me from my eyes and lips.

We got on the tube at Tottenham Court and headed up the Northern line to Highgate. I started to sober up a bit as we walked from the station to his flat. We had to cut through the woods and walk in near darkness for a bit. That was the first time I felt unsure about him. There was something in his voice as it spoke from the darkness. All he was talking about was some silly story involving one of his colleagues at the job centre he worked at nearby, but it made me think he was acting something out, like he'd performed all this before. I could've run off home there and then, but I thought of the drink, and of the sex, and kept walking.

When we got inside his flat, there was strong smell of off-food like he hadn't emptied his bin in a while. Everything was tidy — the carpets were clean, the surfaces polished — so I didn't say anything about it. There were a few mirrors along both sides of the hall and, as we walked through it, we were reflected, over and over, so that it felt like we weren't the only people in his flat that night.

We headed into his kitchen. There was a large pot of curry resting on an old stove. Its fragrant stench seemed to drown out the odd smell in the rest of the house. He offered me some and I was quick to say yes as I hadn't eaten a proper meal the whole day. He lit the gas on the ring under the pot and fixed me a vodka coke while the curry heated. He passed me the drink and I took a sip – my throat stung with how much vodka he'd poured in, but I didn't complain. The quicker I felt relaxed, the better.

Once the curry had reheated, he ladled me a full bowl with some cold rice. He didn't take any for himself. I shovelled a large spoonful into my mouth and was hit with the richness of flavour and spice.

What's this? Pork? I asked. The meat was poor quality. Rubbery.

Aye. Ye like it?

Yeah, it's nice, I lied. I ate all the rice and left the rest of the meat untouched.

He asked me about my Psychology degree. He'd read a lot of the theory — more than I ever had. I tried to impress him by speaking about Lacan and Jung, but he laughed at me when I pronounced Jung with a 'J' and I gave up trying. He had his own theories about human behaviour. He spoke about them like they were hard facts and didn't seem open to them being wrong in any way. I didn't have the knowledge or command of language back then to argue with him. I just poured myself more drinks, each one stronger than the last, and nodded my head at all the right moments. I could feel myself getting more and more drunk, but he didn't seem to be as affected, except for his speech which became more relaxed and Scottish. Thankfully my father's from Moray, so I had little trouble in understanding him.

In the light of the small lampshade above us, his steel-rimmed glasses glinted like a knife. I wanted to take them off to see what he looked like without them. I imagined he'd appear younger, but not necessarily more attractive. It didn't really matter either way. I'd drank enough not to care. I put my feet up on his legs and he lightly stroked my shins.

When was yer first sexual experience? he asked. He'd been speaking about Freud and I hadn't been paying much attention.

Just last year. When I was seventeen. Some guy I met in a club I'd snuck into. Nothing to write home about, I sighed. You?

When I was eight, he said. He was waiting for my reaction and smiled when he got it. I was playing doon the shorie, alone, or so I thought. It was a fine day, but the waves were rough and I swam oot too far and nearly droont.

He stopped there. Out from his pockets, he placed down his keys and wallet before rustling out a packet of fags and a lighter. He lit one up, took a long draw and puffed the smoke out above my head.

And then I woke up choking, he continued. An older boy had resuscitated ma, but he was up and on his feet as soon as I came roon. He ran awa oot o sight afore I realised fit he'd done. There was a string of white liquid across ma belly. I didna ken fit it was at the time. I just washed it aff wie seawater and went hame.

I took me a few seconds to understand everything he was saying, but once it registered, I felt like he was lying. I don't know exactly how I could tell. Maybe it was because he couldn't look directly at me as he said it, but up at the ceiling, as though searching his mind.

Oh god, that's crazy, I said to please him. My speech was slurring and my back started to ache. Can we sit somewhere a bit more comfy?

Aye, just heid through to the living room. I'll clean this up, he said before staring hard at the half-full bowl. He snatched it up and scraped the remaining food into the bin.

I walked through to the lounge. I'd almost become accustomed to the weird smell, but it was worse in here when I sat down. I was about to get up to go back through to the kitchen when he came to the door. He had his top off and in his hands. Given how thin he was, his torso and arms were strangely muscular.

I'm just gan to hae a quick shower. Just mak yoursel at hame, he said. He left the doorway and I heard the boiler clicking in his kitchen.

I wandered about the room. He had a good record collection from what I remember. It was A-Z in a box by the record player. The one that sat on the turntable read Elvis Presley in silver letters. I switched it on and placed the needle down on the record. There was a crackling noise for a few seconds before 'Are You Lonesome Tonight?' began playing.

I continued to snoop around. There was a small wardrobe in the corner of the room. It seemed out of place in here, like it belonged in a bedroom for storing clothes. It was made of dark wood with a gloss finish. I tried to open it, but it was locked and the small keyhole was empty.

I headed back through to the kitchen. All the other doors in the hall were closed. Water was running behind one of them. I picked his keys off the kitchen table and sifted out a small, chunky black key with an ornate carving at one end. Back in the lounge, I placed it into the keyhole and turned the lock slowly, making sure that the rest of the keys didn't jangle. I stayed still and listened — the water was still running in the bathroom. I opened the wardrobe.

Inside, there were a few jackets hanging from a rail. Nothing out of the ordinary. But the smell was even worse and I knew that this was where it was coming from. I bent down and drew the jackets to one side like a curtain. There were three black bin bags, all tied shut. I slowly reached out to feel one of them. I stroked my fingertips across the black plastic and felt something cold yet familiar. It was like touching a joint of meat. I gripped onto one end and quickly flinched back away from the cupboard with a small yelp — even though I couldn't see it, I knew I'd grabbed onto the cold rigid fingers of a lifeless human hand.

The music stopped.

Fit ye think ye'r deeing? a voice said behind me.

He was stood there in nothing but a pair of white Y-fronts, his trouser belt gripped in his hands. Before I dared make a move, he leapt towards me, wrapped the belt round my throat and pulled me, like a dog on a leash, out of the room. I tried to scream, but choked instead with the force of the leather against my neck. In the mirrors of the hall, I could see my face purpling as he dragged me through to the bathroom. The next breath I took was when he released his grip on the belt before replacing it with his bare hands. He hoisted me up over the rim of the bathtub and dunked my head under the tepid water that was still pouring in from both taps. My vision blurred with both the water and faint-headedness — all I could make out was the dark ellipse of the bath plug against the white ceramic tub. Bubbles escaped through my nose and water rushed into my body. I fought back as hard as I could, kicking and flailing my arms with the last of my energy.

I got a hold of his crotch and yanked hard. Through the garbled blur of water, I heard a howl of pain. He let go. I leapt upwards, gasping for air. He was sat on the closed toilet seat, cupping his hands round his genitals with his head turned away from me as though shamed.

I ran. Out the bathroom, out the flat, down the stairs, out onto the street and towards the main road. Water seeped from my nose and dripped warmly onto my cold soaking top. I'd never been more thankful to not be wearing heels, nor more thankful to get back to my own flat and bolt the door behind me.

I never went back to the drag club after that night. Soon after, I quit my Psychology degree and London altogether. I moved back to Manchester and worked in bars for a few years until, eventually, I went back to university and studied Education.

I'd been teaching primary school kids for around twenty years when we went on an end-of-term trip to London. It was the first time I'd been there since I left. I couldn't face returning after he was caught and I found out I'd been one of the lucky ones. Found out I'd done nothing to stop him from killing more men.

During the trip, the bus dropped us off at Madame Tussauds first. I had to keep an eye on a group of primary sevens who were too hyper for my liking, but good kids all the same. They ran around taking pictures of each other with the waxworks — one pretended to fight with Muhammad Ali and another held hands with David Beckham. We entered the Chamber of Horrors section and walked past a plaque for Jack the Ripper and a model of Sweeney Todd. At first the kids tried to make each other jump by sneaking about and whispering in each other's ears and prodding sides, but they were soon subdued by the gore of it all. They called me over to a waxwork of someone they'd never heard of. I walked over and read the plaque. I felt my face drain.

DENNIS NILSON

1945 –

'The Muswell Hill Murderer'

Murdered up to 15 young men.

Sentenced in 1983 to life imprisonment

They'd spelled his surname wrong — Anglicised it away from the spelling of his Norwegian father. I looked up at the model of him. The glasses were identical and the style of his clothes were similar to the ones he'd wore on that night in eighty-two, but he looked older than when I met him and the waxy sheen of the skin made him look feverish. Sickly.

I stayed silent as we walked onwards. There was a tightness in my chest. I breathed slowly and kept my shaking hands in my pockets.

When we left and stepped back out onto Marylebone Road, the London air had never smelled so fresh. I felt like I'd been released from some prison and was walking free for the first time.

The rest of the day went ahead as planned: a walk in Regent's park, a theatre tour, dinner at Pizza Hut and then we were all on the bus back to Manchester. Everything happened around me like I wasn't really part of it, like I was watching a slow, plotless film and yearning for the end.

It grew dark as the bus headed northwards and one-by-one all the kids became silent. Although it felt like I'd not done much all day, I was exhausted. I closed my eyes and slept and dreamt...

I was walking in the woods, a faint orange glow of streetlights in the distance and a sliver of moon in the night sky. Instead of sticking to the trodden path, I drifted into the thick of the trees. Branches brushed against my arms and legs, more and more the deeper I went, until I came to a clearing. There was a double mattress in the middle of it with a white duvet and one coverless pillow. Without hesitating, I got in under the blanket and put my head down to rest. Voices began speaking from the darkness; they all sounded male but their words overlapped to the point where everything was incomprehensible. My eyes became accustomed to the darkness enough for me to see dark objects sliding across the white duvet towards me. I realised they were hands reaching out, not to grab at me, but to be held.

There was a tapping at my shoulder and I woke with a start. My hands were trembling and my crotch was soaking wet. I was so glad to be wearing black trousers, but my face burned all the same.

One of the other teachers was staring down at me over the

seat in front. She was frowning above her red-rimmed glasses, most likely annoyed that I'd been sleeping all that time.

That's us John. Time to get home, she said. Y'alright? You don't seem yourself.

At first, I didn't know what to tell her, but then I watched the kids file out of the bus and thought of how their stories ended when they couldn't think of a logical conclusion for what had come before.

Yeah, I said. It was just a dream.

Harry Josephine Giles

ABOLISH THE POLICE

The moon is doing poemy things   and so he takes
a police apart: a police is held   in the silver column
and extracted from himself.   His head, yes, detaches,
but without much drama,   and his arms are peeled with the love
of a Cheestring Original,   gunk-strips inspected
by stubbornly poemy moonlight.   The moon spins the dead police
and the dead police uniform   and the moon vanishes all
the dead police to the dead moon sea   where there is quiet.
'I'm sorry,' says the moon,   'that I never did this before.'
And the people forgive the moon   and let go their poems.

ABOLISH THE POLICE

Of course when I say ‘abolish the police’   I am describing a bird:
bill like a rusted plough,   rump like a loaf of bread,
chin, throat and neck alive   like the mourning surface
of a washing up bowl.   What else could it mean but that this bird’s flanks
are expanding   like the breath of a minor mountain, and what else
can describing a bird achieve   but the bloody end of all police?

ABOLISH THE POLICE

I told my friend the poet   with the care of a non-stick pan
that his behaviour   was making women uncomfortable
and that I wanted to help.   He ran away in gulps, said
he might as well die,   that he was off somewhere good
to die. I chased him down the street;   the soundtrack
was old trombones and struck strings;   I sung
'please stop'   and lines from photocopied zines.
He did not stop.   I called the police. I watched the police
make him stop with two cars   and guide him inside.
They put a lock on him   so that he would not die.

ABOLISH THE POLICE

You say that my violence   disturbs you.
I press   blue fingernails
in an arc   around your left nipple
and through,   cupping the heart
from above,   and this feels
to both of us   like truffles melting
against the roofs   of our mouths.
'Do you imagine,'   I say,
'That I   am not disturbed?
I wish I could imagine   an end
to police   untouched by revenge.'
'Try harder,' you say,   slicing a poem
across my palm,   a neat cut
that you take   into your huge mouth,
eyes sharp   with unwanted wealth.

Ciara Maguire

THE MIDDLE OF EVERYTHING

It was a Saturday and the queue for the toilets was even more rammed than usual. Bodies damp with sweat and spilled drinks pressed against each other as the line slowly shuffled forward. Abi craned her neck to measure the distance to the front of the queue and wished she hadn't downed three vodka lemonades in such quick succession.

It was her first night out in a while. She used to be here three nights a week and was on first name terms with the bouncers, could recognise other regulars by a glimpse of their blue hair gleaming under the strobe lights, and could swear she had memorised the same tracklist of pop and R'n'B songs that the DJ rotated through each night. Now, Abi could no longer recognise the young scene queens and instead felt a sort of maternal fondness for them, laughing and showing off to each other in their muscle tees and cacophony of bad tattoos. Six months away from the clubs shouldn't have felt like such a long time, but in gay time she was essentially retired.

She had come at the insistence of her best friend Rosa. 'Don't be a boring bitch,' Rosa had said. 'Lauren is desperate to go to a gay club for her birthday and if you don't come, it's just me, Lauren and Greg and all their straight pals. I refuse to be the only gay at the gay club. Please, Abi.'

There was a sudden surge forward in the queue and Abi felt her foot connect with another foot headed in the opposite direction.

'Fuck. Sorry.'

'Abi?'

'Oh my god. Poppy.'

She looked the same, except her hair was longer and bleached blonde, and the nose ring that used to get perpetually tangled in Abi's hair was gone.

'How have you been? When did you get back?'

Abi and Poppy had dated briefly a while back, although dating might have been too grand a term for their relationship. They had met, as most modern dykes did, on Tinder. They met up at a nice bar that had mood lighting and expensive cocktails, and after one drink had headed to the nearest lesbian bar that favoured fluorescent strip lights and £1 shots.

Poppy was fun. She had just quit her job in anticipation of moving to Australia and had three weeks of freedom to burn before she left. They spent their first night moving from bar to bar, talking and laughing. Poppy shared the story of the hamster she accidentally killed by dropping her DJ mixer on it.

'It was awful. I never played again,' she said solemnly, as Abi tried her best to keep a straight face.

Eventually they wound up in a basement bar where they were the only women there and the youngest by a good thirty years. A melancholy drag queen in a yellow dress sang Kate Nash. As Abi shot Poppy a raised eyebrow and stifled an awkward giggle, Poppy grabbed her face and kissed her, and Abi felt something twist inside her as she closed her eyes.

The next few weeks had passed in a haze of gin, sunshine and sex. Being with Poppy was easy and there was none of the usual cloud of commitment hanging over them, with the knowledge that soon they would be separated by an entire world. When the time came for Poppy to leave, there were no grand emotional goodbyes. They stood in Abi's doorway.

'You better keep in touch.' Poppy warned.

'You know I will.'

Abi smiled, hoping that she wouldn't just start crying instead.

Ten minutes later Abi's phone buzzed: *I hear nudes are a great cure for plane sickness.* She laughed.

They had, true to their word, kept in touch, at first swapping letters covered in stickers, Poppy sending postcards from each new town. But after a few months the postcards from Poppy had stopped and their Facebook exchanges were kept sweet but short. And now, here was Poppy in the flesh, tanned and grinning, glitter covering her eyelids and speckled across her arms and chest.

'I got back a few weeks ago. I'm only here for a couple of months, I'm planning a trip to Canada in the New Year.'

Abi felt a flutter of disappointment at the news Poppy wasn't back for good.

'Oh, check you! Canada, that's so exciting.'

'I know. I can't wait. Australia was amazing but far too fucking hot, my poor Scottish skin couldn't handle it.'

'Well, you look great. Honestly. What happened to your nose ring?'

Poppy touched her hand to her nose. 'You're going to laugh, but I lost it when I was diving with sharks.'

'Of course you did. What a gap year cliche.'

'I know, there's probably a wee clownfish swimming about wearing it now.'

'Or a gay white shark.'

'I see your jokes haven't improved then.'

Abi laughed and gave her a gentle shove, when the girl behind them coughed loudly.

'Sorry, this catch up is very cute, but some of us really need a piss.'

Poppy threw Abi a look and turned to the girl. 'Yeah, no problem.' She touched her wrist and Abi felt an old familiar kick of chemistry. 'Find me later, okay?'

Poppy turned and disappeared into the crowd.

Abi left the bathroom and felt herself immediately enveloped by the throngs of people tangled and dancing in the dim lights of the club. She pushed her way through to where she had left her friends, only to find that in the 15 minutes or so she had been gone, Rosa had somehow gotten infinitely more drunk and was now swinging her t-shirt over her head as she jumped up and down, screeching along to the Rihanna remix that was playing.

'AAAAABBBBIIII!!!' she screamed as Abi approached them, flinging her arms around her and kissing her cheek. 'Where have you been? You missed that Eurovision banger, none of this lot knew the words.' Lauren and Greg were leaned against a pillar, looking decidedly more sober and mildly embarrassed.

'Sorry, I was in the toilets. Guess who I bumped into?'

'Oooh. Sam? Hannah? Zoe?'

Abi interrupted, releasing this game could go on for a while. 'Poppy.'

'That girl who went to Australia? She was cute! Is she back now?'

Abi glanced around, wondering if Poppy was here or upstairs having a smoke. 'Yeah, kind of.'

The night passed as nights out with Rosa usually did. She bought them round after round of cheap and sour shots, staining their tongues blue and coating their fingers in a sugary sticky film. They danced till they were out of breath and collapsed into a booth, Rosa's breath hot and boozy on Abi's neck as she leant her head on her shoulder. As the lights came up, Lauren and Greg approached with two plastic pint cups of water.

'Here, steamers, drink these before you leave.'

'So sensible,' slurred Rosa, reaching for the water.

'Are you coming?' asked Lauren.

'Yeah, two secs,' said Rosa, pulling her jacket on. 'Abi, you wanna head back with us?'

'I'm okay. I think I'll walk and get some fresh air.'

Rosa rolled her eyes as she climbed out of the booth.

'You're mad. Text me when you're home safe though.' She leaned forward to kiss Abi on the cheek before they walked away. Abi stayed in the booth a few more moments, sipping her water. She pressed into a droplet on the table, watching it bloom out from under her fingertips.

'That's the thing about staying til the end of the night,' said a familiar voice. Poppy, standing over her, smiling. 'There's only the weirdoes left.'

It was morning. Sun streamed through the thin orange curtains and cast a soft sleepy glow across the room. She could hear distant hammering and workmen calling to each other in the shared gardens outside. She looked over at Poppy, still fast asleep, glitter now mingling with the smudged make up streaked across her face. She was really fucking beautiful. Abi sat up, pulling the duvet over her knees and shifting closer to Poppy so their skin was still touching. On the wall was a faded poster from a Rae Spoon gig. Abi recognised it as one she had been to, but she didn't know Poppy then. She thought of them in the same space, listening to the same music, probably drinking the same cheap wine from plastic cups. She always wished she had known Poppy longer. It felt like a cruel twist of fate that they'd lived in the same city for three years but only met three weeks before she moved away.

On the bedside table sat a small stack of zines. Abi shuffled through them, picking one out. '2 FUCKED 2 FURIOUS: STILL SEXUALLY DYSFUNCTIONAL IN SEX-POSITIVE QUEER SCENES.' She flicked through the pages. She and Poppy had spent many late nights in this room, gazing at the ceiling and going over the intricacies of the queer community, their lives and experiences, and how it all meshed together in ways that could make their heads hurt and hearts full in equal measures.

Poppy stirred beside her and rubbed her eyes, transferring the glittery mascara mess to her fists.

'Fuck. First rule of drinking and still having your life together: remember to take your make-up off before bed.' She groaned. 'Coffee?'

'Yes please.'

Poppy leaned over to kiss Abi and felt her smiling. It felt familiar and sweet, like the honey and butter sandwiches she ate as a child.

Poppy went into the bathroom and sat down to pee. She noticed the tiny bugs crawling across the wall. One thing she hadn't missed about this flat was the impenetrable damp that made her posters peel off the wall and the smell that couldn't quite be masked by the Ikea scented candles she lit around the place. She reached out and traced the journey of one of the bugs before squashing it with her finger. Her vegan activist flatmates wouldn't be pleased to know how often she did this. It felt nice to know Abi was in her bed, only two walls away. She had thought of her often while she was away. After a string of bad relationships, Abi had been her first glimpse of something that just felt good. Most of her exes worked in bars and clubs, and the appeal of free drinks and lazy mornings in bed would begin to fade after realising she spent more time than she liked holding hair back over toilets spattered with vomit, or missing daylight entirely when they didn't surface till after five, most days. Abi was different from the start. She was genuinely excited to see her, waited for her outside work with coffee and one quid carnations before their third date. They swapped books with their favourite passages underlined, watched the worst films they could find on the Netflix LGBTQ section and shared their grand theories on the meaning of life.

Poppy liked herself so much better when she was with Abi. She felt spontaneous and fun, and she didn't have to force herself. But the timing was off. Two weeks before they matched on Tinder, in what was definitely a forced attempt at fun, she'd bought a one-way ticket to Melbourne. Three years worth of call centre wages gone in an instant, and the prospect of sunny beaches instead of eight hour days under fluorescent lights was laid out before her like a dazzling beacon of opportunity.

Her visions of early morning swimming in the sea and days

spent soaking in the sun hadn't quite worked out. The first few months were something close to fun, but she quickly realised that wanting to enjoy something was different than actually enjoying it. She'd followed some friends she met in her hostel along the coast, camping and blowing her savings on cheap cocktails and expensive brunches before ending up at a farm where they could stay for free in exchange for a few hours' labour each day. Except it turned out a 'few hours' was more like twelve, and after a few days lying in an un-air-conditioned hut dying of sunstroke, her arms burnt red and peeling, Poppy decided to give up on her Aussie dream and head back to Glasgow.

She flushed and went over to the sink where she grabbed a pack of cleansing wipes. She exhaled as the cool, damp wipe touched her skin. Maybe she did have a hangover after all.

She had kept to herself since she had got home. She tried not to think of things in such black and white terms — everything happens for a reason, et cetera — but she couldn't help feeling embarrassed that she'd only lasted five months, couldn't even make it halfway into her year-long epic. She decided to take a few months to lick her wounds before she embarked on her second attempt at a real adventure. She stuck a quote from Jack Halberstam's 'Queer Art of Failure' onto her mirror in a particularly self-pitying moment.

'It's fine,' she told herself. 'It's my duty as a lesbian to fail. I'm not aligning myself with corporate ideas of success.' Bumping into Abi on her first night out since she was back felt like another kind of meant-to-be.

When Poppy returned to her room with two mugs of coffee, she saw that Abi had fallen back asleep. Her back was exposed, the rest of her tucked into the green duvet. Poppy sat the mugs on her bedside table and crawled back into bed, feeling the warmth from Abi's sleeping body creep out to embrace her. She traced the muscles on Abi's back, smoothing out the tension between her shoulder blades. One of the things she had liked so much about Abi was how she had walked around her flat in just her oversized black shorts, topless and brazen like a boy. She seemed so blasé about her body, didn't connect it to any trauma or neuroses. She felt envious of that kind of freedom.

'You're back,' Abi mumbled, waking slowly and scrabbling to sit up.

'I have coffee.' Poppy handed her a mug and Abi felt the warmth spread through her fingertips.

'Mmm. The first caffeine of the day is such a beautiful thing.'

'I'm really glad I bumped into you last night, you know.'

'Me too. I've thought of you a lot. It's tragic but the first few weeks after you left I was so sad. I just wandered around Queens Park by myself, listening to Mitski on repeat.'

'Wow, that is tragic.'

They laughed and Poppy let her head relax onto Abi's shoulder.

'Isn't it funny how it feels like no time has passed at all now that we're here together?'

'It is. But I also think our connection is different. Or maybe it's different for all queer people.'

'What, time?' said Abi.

'Yeah. Our lives move in different ways, we don't really adhere to typical timelines, do we? Especially in relationships.'

'Well, it certainly explains the lesbian U-Haul phenomenon.'

'Exactly. Queer temporality. Queer women connectivity. I'll make up a term for it, write a queer theory book on it all.' Poppy said.

'Make sure to dedicate it to me.'

'Of course. I won't forget you when I'm famous.'

Poppy smiled and downed the last of her coffee.

'But we have time now. A little of it.'

'So what are we going to do with it?'

Abi paused. 'Do you want to go to the beach?'

'The beach? In Scotland, in November?'

'Come on. It's sunny outside. We've been separated by the sea for long enough. We should go and visit it together.'

'So poetic. How can I resist?'

They exited the train platform and began walking towards the promenade. In typical Scottish style, the weather had turned during their half hour train ride and now it was pissing it down, the soft morning sun replaced by grisly grey clouds. But despite the weather, when they arrived in front of the sea, it was calm, froth licking the shore as the waves rolled in.

'It's not quite Australia,' Abi remarked.

'No, and I couldn't be more glad.' Poppy looked around her, the Isle of Arran a sunken rock on the horizon in front of her, the row of derelict chip shops and entertainment palaces behind them, shut for the season. Unsurprisingly, they were entirely alone.

She looked back at Abi and realised she was stripping down to her underwear.

'Are you mad?'

'Maybe. Come on. It'll make us feel alive.'

Poppy hesitated, then took off her trainers, stuffing her socks inside them and praying the tide wouldn't come in anytime soon as she peeled off her jeans and t-shirt too.

Abi grinned and grabbed her hand. Without speaking, they started running towards the sea, screaming as the freezing waves slapped their ankles, then their knees, then their hips, a thousand tiny pins pricking their bare limbs.

They stood still, clutching each other for balance, their shrieking subsiding and turning to giggling as the shock of the cold dissipated.

'It's so cold, it's so fucking cold,' Abi gasped.

'I can't believe you made me do this.'

'But aren't you so glad you did?'

And Poppy realised she was. She'd flown a thousand miles in search of adventure and fulfilment and here she was, on Troon beach, in the freezing rain, feeling happier than she had in forever. Above them, shafts of light began to beam through the clouds, causing the water to glitter and the salt on their skin to dry.

April Hill

ABBIE

Abbie sounds pale pink,
sunrise soft and airy but
Abbie-love is different from Abbie.

Say, if I come from the soil
then like every living thing I am reaching
Up, and slow-motion chasing,
I am outstretched and beckoning —
you are made to move towards
the nearest source of heat.

Abbie sounds starry,
freckled and watching quietly but
Abbie-love is different from Abbie.
See, I've been reaching for a while and
mountains are rising out of me. Soil
is soft but missing is not and
the ache of love is hard enough to build with.

See, my April-poem isn't big enough
for my Abbie-love and
the paper keeps catching on my peaks. See,
my April-language is earth-bound but
I've been reaching towards
the nearest source of pink.

Abbie sounds like a name,
but Abbie-love is a landscape
without air,
and it's hard to speak.

RAIN

Don't know if
rain has a heart, or if
rain has a feeling, if
r-a-i-n is a set of individual patter-pits
or just one large cacophony of
piTterpAttErRaInRiTterrAttErpAin
if rain is ray-ay-ay-ayn, if
rain is pulsing, is carved out, is fleshy,
if rain has moist chambers fluttering up against
the hard white bone of feeling.

Say if
rain can feel,
surely I can oscillate,
and if rain can pulse,
I can precipitate,
and if rain can hurt,
I can fall, everywhere,
and this poem can drip,
drop,
drip,
,

And if rain has a heart,
it has a body,
and if it has a body,
it has a skin,
and if rain has a skin,
it must have a touch, must have
digits that can dig in deep, deep
in my soil soul and sink,
in and
drip,
,

And if rain has a body it must have eyes,
eyes that blink open blue-grey and
see inside every living thing and
forgive.

HARVEST

Harvest.
Everything was ripe inside me. The flesh
inside my flesh grew firm and green, and I felt
the bud of it, hard, rubbing between my
limbs everywhere I went. I didn't know how
to garden, only to blossom; it never occurred
to me to take it out.

So Harvest.
I trust you with the insides of me. A warning:
the first bite can be very sour, if only
because it's so fresh. You know I wouldn't lie to you.
You know I only want to give you the best.

Harvesting.
This isn't the love poem I thought I would
write. But this isn't the loving I thought I
would do. I thought it would be all about the
flowers; rather it is all about the fruit. I want
my juice to stain the skin around your lips,
my seeds to get stuck between your teeth.

Harvest — harvesting, harvest time, harvest me.
Dig, dig, digging deep. I have been doing it to myself all
week.
Churning over the rich brown of my mind. My fingers

are stained with soil. They smell of soil. Of
the great insides.

Harvest, harvest, harvesting.
Everything is always cycling in me. I belong to the seasons,
just like everything else earth-grown and natural.
Being with her is natural. I need to stop weather-
checking myself. My body knows what it was made for.

But — harvest time. I woke up smelling like you
because you kissed me last night. I wanted to press myself
into all of your white limbs on show. It's nothing poetic,
but you made me so happy that it kept distracting me from
my own endless
growing pains. Between us, there is something else
green and sun-inclined. Say,
let me sing, hear me sing — this is how I sing!
This is my purpose, produce, present of my soul — say,
My soul! Let me share that with you.

Kirsty Logan

STRANGER BLOOD IS SWEETER

Sarah knows she's been fighting or fucking or eating something. Someone.

'Fell,' Juno says, not even trying to hide it, half-smiling with a chipped canine and her left cheek bruised high and deep. She tucks her hands under the breakfast table, away from the unforgiving sunlight. Last week one of her fingers was broken, and she wouldn't say why.

'You were fine when we went to bed.'

'Got up in the night to pee. And fell.'

Sarah says nothing as she puts ointment on Juno's cheek. Not much she can do about the tooth; she's not a dentist.

Everything is fine for a few mornings — no bruises, at least — then Sarah wakes to a bloody pillow.

'Juno!' she says. 'What the hell?'

'Huh? What?' Juno jolts awake, the blood down her jaw crumbling dry.

'Your ear,' Sarah says.

'Oh.' Juno scratches at the blood flakes with her fingernail and they watch bits flutter to the sheets. 'I fell and I forgot about it.'

Sarah dabs at Juno with a damp washcloth. It looks like her ear was pulled down and released, and the very top has ripped away from her head. Once the blood's cleaned off, it's not that bad.

'You should probably have stitches,' Sarah says.

'Can you tape it or something?'

Sarah does her best, then puts away the First Aid kit. She should ask, she knows she should, but she's scared to hear the answer. She's spent years trying to figure out the damage in Juno. She knows it was something — a terrible thing, a darkness that Juno hints at but never explains. She lets her wife have her secrets. Whatever the darkness, Sarah tells herself, it doesn't make them love each other any less. But can you really love someone you don't know?

The next night, Sarah follows Juno.

The place is walking distance, but it's night and it's dark and the whole time in her head Sarah's self-defence teacher is shouting: *Don't walk alone at night! Keys between your fingers! Go for the eyes and the throat!* Sarah pulls her scarf up over her jaw and tries to walk silently.

In the bleaching streetlight she sees Juno, all in black with her fists wrapped in white, disappear into a building she's never noticed before. It looks like a garage or a workshop. It's something harmless. It must be. Secret mechanic training? Extreme metalworking? Stuntwoman training. Roller derby.

Sarah leans against the wall outside, taking deep breaths, getting ready. Though the door is ajar, she can't hear anything from inside the building. She keeps her keys in her clenched fists.

Inside, the building is lit with red emergency lighting. Sarah follows the narrow corridor around. She strains her ears but there's nothing; only a pressure, a held breath. The definite sense of people waiting just around the corner. She emerges into a larger space, and sees the backs of two dozen women looking down at something.

A bell rings. Two staggered thumps, like dropped sandbags. Then a wet thud, a fast exhalation. She sidles through the massed women without looking at any of their faces, not daring to see if any of them is Juno. She comes up short on the lip of a circular pit about eight feet deep. Dirt floor. Bare brick walls.

In the pit two women circle one another, fists raised, knees bent, swaying low. One is holding her left hand oddly, as if the fingers are broken. The other has a lipstick-red smear of blood from her nostrils to her chin.

One feints, the bird-fast dart of a head, but the other doesn't fall for it. A fist below the ribs and she folds, broken hand scuffing the dirt. A kick to the belly, to the shins. She lifts her knees to protect her body. Sarah closes her eyes. The smack of flesh. The sharp smell of blood.

She pushes her way outside and vomits against the wall.

She runs away before Juno can see her. In the shadows, on the way home, she does what she needs to do.

When Juno gets home, Sarah rolls over as if she's just woken up.

'Hey,' she says.

'Hey,' Juno says. 'Just went to the loo,' and this is surely the stupidest lie yet as her skin is nighttime-cold and she's barely caught her breath.

In the darkness, Sarah reaches for her, pushes her hands down, down. Sarah's already wet against Juno's fingers, but it might just be blood.

Sarah stands at the sink and washes the breakfast dishes, looking at the cluster of trees that hides their neighbour's windows. Even in the morning sun, beneath the trees it's all shadow. If she keeps her hands in the water, Juno won't see what's caught under her nails.

'At work the other day we were talking about our favourite stories from when we were kids.' Sarah knows it's clunky and horrible but can't think how else to ask. 'What was your favourite story when you were little?'

'Have you seen my other work bra?' Juno's piling things into her bag, chewing a toast crust. 'The wire's coming out of this one.'

'I don't know that story.'

'What?'

'I said,' Sarah says, turning from the sink, 'what was your favourite –'

'I heard you, Sarah. I don't know, *Chicken Little* or *E.T.* or something. *Hansel and Gretel*, maybe? I liked the gingerbread house. Now can you please tell me if you've seen my bra?'

Sarah dries off and keeps the tea-towel in her hands as she goes to find the bra, which is in the dirty washing basket where Juno left it. The problem is that *Chicken Little* and *E.T.* and *Hansel and Gretel* all suggest very different things. If she liked *Chicken Little*, then she tried to tell someone that a bad thing had happened and they didn't believe her. If it was *E.T.*, then a friend was mistreated and she couldn't save them. *Hansel and Gretel* was the worst of all. Abandoned children and evil mothers and the threat of being eaten, of wanting to eat things you shouldn't eat. There are a few things that Juno doesn't know about Sarah, that she never thinks to ask, and one that Sarah will never tell is that her own favourite story was always *Hansel and Gretel.* When she first heard it, it made her hungry. It still does.

She goes back into the kitchen and hands Juno the bra.

'I can't wear this, Sarah. It's dirty.'

'Why *Hansel and Gretel*?' Sarah asks. 'Are you hungry? Do you want more breakfast?'

'Never mind, I'll just wear the one I've got on.' Juno gives Sarah a distracted kiss and grabs her car keys. 'Later, okay? I'll get dinner.'

But later is no good. She needs to know now. She needs to figure out the appeal of the place where Juno goes. The desire, the goad. It's dizzy and sick and confused, and where is all this coming from? Who is she, really?

The next night, she follows Juno again. Just walking into the place — the red light, the waiting breath — all the blood drops from her brain and her heart thuds in her throat.

She pulls her hood low over the sides of her face and elbows her way through the women to the front, toes right on the edge of the pit. The bell rings.

She watches Juno drop down into the pit. Another woman follows, dreadlocks knotted on top of her head. She raises her fists and Juno lunges, gets in a hit. The woman backs away, shakes her head, her nose dripping blood onto the dirt. Juno bounces back on the balls of her feet, fists protecting her face, elbows protecting her body. The woman kicks out and sweeps Juno's feet from under her. Juno thuds to the ground but lashes out with her feet as she falls and gets the woman in the lower belly and she doubles over and reaches for Juno's hair, slams her head against the ground. Juno's got her fingers in the crook of the woman's elbow and she's pulling, trying to get free, and she lurches up and smacks the underside of the woman's chin with the crown of her head. Someone shouts, they separate, they circle one another with their hands up and their bodies low and their breath fast and hot. The air is heavy with strangers' skin and the smell of blood and the light catches the gleam of eyes and flesh slaps and bodies thud and it's red and black and red and black and red.

The next morning she puts arnica cream on Juno's bruised forearms, she sticks butterfly stitches to Juno's split lip, she splints Juno's fractured toe.

'Clumsy,' Sarah says. 'You're so clumsy, my love.'

Keeping her mouth closed so Juno won't taste what's caught between her teeth, she kisses the broken parts, one by one by one.

The next week, Juno is away for work, and the first night Sarah lies awake in their cold bed. The second night she goes out into the shadows and does what she needs to do. The next night, she goes to the red-lit building and stands at the lip of the pit, watching.

Women punch each other in the face. Women break one

another's fingers. Women get pinned to the ground with knees on their throats and retch in the dirt. Women take punches, have their heads snap back against the wall, get knocked unconscious. Women come away with strands of each other's hair in their fists. One woman forces another into a corner and braces her hands on the wall and kicks the woman in the belly over and over and over.

When Juno gets home, Sarah says: 'I followed you.'

Juno, confused, not sure whether it's a joke. 'On my work trip?'

'No. At night.'

A long pause. 'When?'

'Does it matter?'

'I didn't—'

'Don't lie, Juno.'

'It's not a big deal. It's just — it helps.'

'Helps with what?'

'You know what,' Juno says.

'You like to beat women up?'

'It's not like that.'

'So you like them to beat you up? Do you want me to beat you up?'

'Jesus Christ. I knew you wouldn't understand.'

'Would you — can you stop?'

'I can't, Sarah. I need it.'

'Can you take a break?'

'If you know I need it, why would you ask me to stop?'

'Because I don't want to see it again.'

'So don't follow me.'

'Please. Until I get to know this new version of you. We can't be strangers. Please, Juno.'

'Okay,' Juno says. 'Okay.' And as she pulls her close and kisses her, Sarah tastes the blood from Juno's split lip. Sarah kisses harder.

That night Sarah makes spag bol, and they eat it with a bottle of red wine in front of the TV, mopping up the sauce with garlic bread. The whole evening, it's nice. It's clean. It's gentle. No smell of blood, no smack of flesh.

Later they make love, and that's nice and clean too. Sarah is the little spoon, and holds Juno's arm around her tight, but not too tight. Nice. Clean.

Juno waits until she thinks Sarah is asleep, then she slips out of bed and wraps her fists and goes out alone.

Sarah hears the front door click shut and counts to a hundred. She goes out into the shadows and she finds the thing she wants. She fights it. And she fucks it. And she eats it.

Jack Bigglestone

PRACTICE

Towards each other, men ran, a rush
Of eager limbs, arms waited until hard-embraced
Met with neck safely cupped to waist
Shoulder below rib pushed out a hush
Of breath — two fall so others must crush
Over their bodies, a bower, arched and interlaced
The coy game of running to be chased
Left them, muscles taut, panting faces flush

Now crowding along benches all squeeze
Hands on strong bruised backs where sweat drips
Mud crusted tees like used armour strips
Foreign fingers tend swelling lips with care
In steam-close air, stiff roughness bends to ease
Answering pleas of bodies laid bare

Sandra Alland

SMUDGED

Shania could apply mascara in the dark, sculpt their cheeks while on the phone, and paint lipstick in the horizontal rain of a Glasgow winter. They took after their mother in such things.

Shania remembered the night Mum got lifted because a council worker suspected her of terrorism for putting out the wrong recycling. Despite no sheets, shoes or sleep, their mother had emerged model-perfect from the cells the next day. As Mum told it, she cat-walked past gaping, racist police on her way directly to the council, where she filed a very loud and effective complaint about the new 'spy on your neighbour' guidelines. Aye, Shania's family was gifted at glam under pressure.

Except Shania was pants at putting on eyeliner. One side tilted up at the corner of their brown left eye, while the other flew even and straight to the edge of their hazel right eye. And it all smeared, raccoon-like. *Bandit Eyes*, Mum called them, which was also a way of avoiding saying their name.

Upon inspection with their magnifying glass, Shania could see that it was indeed their left eye that was guilty of an upward tilt. They wiped at it with a towel, turning the fabric a lovely cobalt. How many times until they should give up? How much would their make-up matter in Glasgow's posh and white West End? As a blind genderqueer from Pollokshaws, they found it hard to care. But they redrew the line anyway, for themself.

Little did Shania know as they sat squinting into their mirror, today none of their preparations would matter at all. Today, Shania would put on their best red jacket, smooth down their favourite charity-shop skirt, and leave the tenement on the way to their date, only to meet Death in the close and be forever waylaid.

Of course, Death did know about the meeting. She was nervous about it, so nervous her freckled white hands fumbled with the buttons of her robe.

Death wasn't her real name. Her name was Penny, though the others just called her Pen. Pen had been doing the Soul Grabbing gig for a few years now, and was thinking of getting out. The hours were shite for one, and they were constantly sending her to Govanhill and Drumchapel, to the poorest and least likely to afford chiropractors, organic food, therapists or certain kinds of surgeries. She felt like a right traitor preying on her own people. Why couldn't she grab Iain Duncan Smith or Theresa May? Or Donald Trump when he was around golfing on stolen land.

The others didn't seem to notice. When they had their monthly night off of grabbing, the whole group walked gleefully up the Necropolis, singing shoulder-to-shoulder among the tombs. Pen always lagged behind their silhouetted hoods and robes, looking up at the moon and wondering why anyone would want to take a soul for so little in return. It reminded her of when she was alive and working for minimum wage at an Edinburgh theatre that made millions off shite musicals yet somehow passed as a charity. A theatre that paid its staff pish on zero-hour contracts to sell tickets to Aladdin starring white actors with spray tan.

But Pen hadn't been qualified for much, could only work certain hours because of chronic pain, and wasn't getting any younger. So she had gritted her teeth when she saw her weekly pay. Gritted them harder when customers called her 'young lady', even though she was 42 years old and a strong contender for the farthest thing from a lady in south Edinburgh.

But what really got her then, too, was the cheerfulness of her co-workers. Anti-trans banter, casual racism and no holiday pay were okay, because the boss gifted the staff a bowl of fruit once a week. It was so thoughtful, her colleagues said. It felt like a family. There were worse problems in the world, but this was one of those things that made Pen lose hope. What people would justify to feel worthy, safe. Loved.

'At least she cares,' Shania said to their mirror. 'Even if she won't tell people about me.' They were thinking about their girlfriend, Melanie, and as soon as they spoke they knew they were talking pure bullshit.

Those were the last words Shania said to their mirror. They were already walking past their mother in the kitchen (*Bandit Eyes, where you off to?*) and out the door, and in two minutes and 37 seconds they would be in the close with Death. They would never make it to Melanie's, where they planned to break up with her for not learning the word 'transmisogyny'. For roughly placing her hands on body parts she had never asked the names for.

Shania looks like a right film star, Pen thought, as she watched them turn on a shiny heel into the close. *Not helpful.* Grabbers saw in black and white, which was meant to decrease attachment to the human world and bland away connection. But as Pen put up her hood in the required fashion before a taking, she noticed that in black and white Shania just looked more radiant. Their colourless walk made their clothes shimmer, their white cane glow, their uniquely-applied eyeliner pop in contrast with their hijab. As Pen became Death, she was more drawn to Shania instead of less.

Death suddenly felt ridiculous in her ill-fitting robe as she stood pale, Catholic and ginger in the middle of a Glasgow close. What was she like, about to attack a blind Muslim in broad, overcast daylight? Surely if there was a god controlling all of this, he/she/they/zie would find this sort of thing distasteful. The other grabbers never questioned, but she was certain there had to be a rulebook somewhere, or at least someone in charge. The afterlife couldn't be just as pointless and unfair.

Before Death knew it, Shania was practically on top of her. Instinctively Death did that embarrassing thing which she knew from her theatre disability awareness training was the absolute worst thing you could do when a blind person was coming at you waving their stick. She weaved back and forth herself, causing Shania to pause and lose their rhythm, unsure which way to go.

Then it was like Death was trying to win a medal for offensiveness. She didn't do one wrong thing; she did all the wrong things, in succession. When it seemed she would choose a side and walk in that direction (her left, Shania's right), she instead moved again to the centre. And she stood there, rooted, blocking the way. Then, at the exact moment Shania made a move to go around her, Death also jerked to life and moved in the same direction. She blushed at Shania's exasperated sigh when they collided.

It was a disaster of arms, legs, white stick and flowing fabrics. As they fell, Death in her rising panic yelled into Shania's pissed-off face — 'Would you be okay with all of this if I gave you a Granny Smith apple? A bunch of grapes? Would you go gentle into that good night?'

Oh God, Death thought. *Not only am I yelling nonsense but also I just quoted* that *poem. What is wrong with me?*

Shania was quiet and still. They grasped the gravity of the situation, if not the specifics. Death, however, was losing her grip entirely. She threw off her hood, wondering how it was possible that she had brought all her ableist bullshit into the next life, how she hadn't unlearned anything, how in the end (was there an end?) she was just as limited as her non-disabled co-workers, both human and grabber.

Fury welled in Death. She was convinced if she hadn't had a heart attack at 42 years old, that if she hadn't been grabbed so early, she would've overcome this shite that had somehow followed her like the smell of rotten bananas across to the other side, or at least the underside.

Death looked at her watch. She was late now, too. She'd never been late before, in life or death, and wasn't sure what it would mean. Was inaction a crime? Could she decide to leave untouched all that beauty and potential, the smell of kindness? And what would happen if she did? Her hands were scraped. Could she say she'd been injured, or attacked by Shania who then got away? Who would she have to justify herself to? Would she be forced to come back tomorrow and try again? Or worse — would someone else come?

Death pictured Eric, James, Kirsty. All the mediocrity of her grabber family. She felt ill at the thought of any of them covering Shania's face with their hands and pulling. That painful yank up and out, then the falling of the shell; Shania reduced to a flopping doll. The inside of Death's skull flashed and glimmered with the terror of it.

'I hate fruit.'

Death opened her eyes to the black and white world of Shania dusting themself off above her.

'Especially bananas,' they added. 'I cannae stand the stench of them. I prefer chocolate cake with double chocolate icing. Also olives with cheese.'

'Oh,' replied Death, scrambling to pull her hood back onto her buzzing head.

'But to answer your question, no,' said Shania. 'Not even if it was cheese you were offering. Camembert, paneer, ackawi or manchego. I'm no ready and I wilnae go gently. Fuck that.'

Peering down at Death, Shania could only decipher a pale smudge. They were unsure what was happening, but they could tell this awkward ginger person wasn't a threat. Plus, it had been ages since anyone asked them something so deep, even if it had been terribly framed.

Shania held out a well-manicured hand. 'Oh god, now my only thought is manchego.'

Then Death was accepting Shania's hand, and they were off across the Auldhouse Burn and over the fences of the private golf club and past crumbling farmhouses. They waded the Brock and Levern, waving at the castle their dads both played in as children but not together, never together back then. They stared sombrely as they passed the hospital where people with mental ill-health were locked up even in 2018, mourning how governments always forced poor people further and further out and apart. They talked about community and how they yearned for it, and about all the cheeses they could name and the cheeses they couldn't name, and about how Scottish children would have thought cheese was gold in 1915 and 1950 and under Thatcher and probably a lot of them still did. They remembered cheese toasties.

And the only sounds were two voices made of hope, and a distant rumble of clouds with bellies of black joy, soon to burst forth and cover it all.

Etzali Hernández

deathless

Another year without your voice,
bright words, tongue in cheek, mellow laugh.
Your voice that hit my chest like a burning arrow.

My skin is fractured
like your favourite porcelain
dropped on the floor.
There's a dull thud when someone else touches me,
my birthmarks ache for you and you only.

My heart has abandoned me:
something dark is in its place,
dull and emotionless,
like a hardened raisin.

High echoes in endless space,
glint in the distance,
webs in the corners,
ice in my throat.

Only memory,
every detail on repeat.
Only blame for myself
and not
for this fucking border.

Yellow happiness.
Ghastly self-love.
Snail's resignation.
Thunderstruck depression.

You have become
a cave of memory:
stalactites hanging,
geysers erupting,
lava scorching my insides.

This is all I have:
a faded image of you.
But then in a sigh:
the warmth of your silky hands,
the sound of your hearty laugh,
the brown of your gleamy eyes,
the dimples on each side of your cheeks.

And I hold tight on to this, like when I was a small child
holding your hand.

ANCESTRY

I know this name and this skin are a loan from my mother,
grandmother and great grandmother
I have been living a borrowed and privileged life.
I don't share the visceral pain and unutterable agony
brought by los hombres blancos

I only share what they left behind them

a poison in the depths of our genetic memory,
a brutal and perpetual war that forced grandma out to a place
indifferent to her traditions, to her womanhood, to her divine existence,
whitewash over our eyes

all of it running through me.

Us, the unwanted: mayas, aztecas, olmecas, toltecas,
purépechas, teotihuacanas, zapotecas, mixtecas, tlaxcaltecas,
totonacas, huastecas, chichimecas, indígenas norteamericanas
y esclavas africanas.

El hombre blanco thought that by annihilating us he could tame us

Ha!

We have endured you.

We come from what feeds the earth
We come from where the rivers begin
We come from fire, wood and ashes
We come from the sun, the moon and the stars
We come from the breath of the goddesses

And as the saying tells:

Trataron de enterrarnos, pero no sabían que éramos semillas.

daughters of god

7 women are murdered every day in México:
Fluids all over the bed
Blood on the wall
Bones crushed into powder
Her marrow destroyed in the name of god and men.

Did god ask him to kill you?
What were his reasons? loving, caring and trusting too much?
being different? being a puta?
what does all that even mean?

Ama a tu prójimo como a ti misma was the prayer,
at my all-girls catholic high school.

If I had loved everyone the way I was taught,
my love would be dust and ashes,
a devoted rosary of self-hate and self-destruction,

I remember being told:
-el lugar de una mujer es en su casa-
-un buen marido es todo lo que necesitas-
-ser mamá es lo mejor que te puede pasar en tu vida-

and with those words resonating
the possibility of being other than
a housewife, straight or a mother
was totally out of the question.

It took an oversea journey
to realize what I always knew:
I am
vanished from
your concept
of womanhood.

I am reclaiming the parts of me that you have beaten,
drowned, burned, raped, diluted and erased.

Now, I love with the intensity I was taught:
Ama a tu prójime, como a ti misme.

what I see when I see you

Your love is a minefield. When I'm close to you my bloodstream explodes into microscopic units of myself: cytoplasm, nucleus, plasma membrane, mitochondria, ribosomes, centrioles.

warm, cold, warm, cold

Your hands have experienced hardness. I feel the roughness of your skin on mine. I want you to trace the curve of my breast, hips and belly button. I cannot stop thinking about what it feels to have your lips on me. Do you like my taste?

soft, wet, soft, wet

Your brown eyes that have seen more wonders and sorrows than anyone else I know. Your soul makes me move in an unconscious rhythm when you look at me and I wonder what do you see when you see me and I see you afraid of being loved.

sweet, sour, sweet, sour

Your burgundy lips, your mouth bursting into a waterfall of smiles. The smoothness of your voice that carries the echo of your experiences. When I hear you talking my body vibrates with you, like a pebble making a ripple. Put your lips on mine and feel the love of our ancestors pouring in.

rhythm, tone, rhythm, tone

Your love is a minefield. When I'm close to you my bloodstream explodes into microscopic units of myself: cytoplasm, nucleus, plasma membrane, mitochondria, ribosomes, centrioles.

Felicity Anderson-Nathan

FORGIVE THE RAIN

I have been trying to count the types of rain. It helps me to hold on to you.

There is the smirr which glittered your hair, and the sudden torrents which you called monsoons despite the cold. There is the horizontal drive which Glasgow is most famous for: it hit our bedroom window like machine gun fire and woke you up in the night. Well-meaning tourist guides tell visitors to bring umbrellas but we know better. This is a city which eats umbrellas for breakfast and leaves their carcasses out on the street. The rain which reminds me the most of you is the fine mist which hangs in the cloudless air. In spring, the setting sun catches it like a city wide prism and every drop refracts in every colour. The sun suspends the rain and the rain reminds the sun to slow down.

It was none of these when I took Moira in.

I was half asleep, tangled in my sheets and dreaming of thunderheads, when the door buzzed. It's never good news in the middle of the night. There was that one time when it was your mum, calling from the hospital. I remember thinking it was strange she did that — your dad was stable, and they wouldn't even let you visit him until morning. You were awake at 3am, painting huge grey canvasses the way you always did when you were worried. Our families were very different; my mum was in the ground before I even knew she was sick.

It was in that thick part of the night where everyone had drifted apart to their own world, the bars long closed, any partiers still awake huddled at home with back-of-the-cupboard bottles. The storm outside was the kind that blows in off the Atlantic and shakes the roof tiles and floods the drains. A downpour which had lasted all the day before, turning the streets into treacherous brown rivers, and filling up wellies like jugs at a tap. It was a terrible night to be outside.

I was too tired to be polite.

'What are you doing here?'

Moira didn't have an umbrella, of course. Or a raincoat, or sturdy boots. She was wearing something black and flimsy, buried under a hoodie.

'I remembered you lived around here,' she said. She didn't even have the decency to look miserable. She was soaked but she stood perfectly upright, that smile on her face. The same one I remembered. 'Want to catch up?'

'Come in then,' I said.

Behind me: footsteps, the drip of rainwater on tile.

'You've changed things,' she said.

'Most of it was Vi,' I said. 'She loved her statement walls.'

'I suppose it was,' she agreed, wiggling out of her hoodie. It was saturated and smelled like it had been used to unclog a drain. I went to hang it up but turned instead to the cupboard with the dryer.

'We weren't really together long enough to get into home decor,' she said, laughing. Like she'd told a joke. Her hand was suddenly on my shoulder. 'Thanks Indra. You've always been so decent.'

The machine started up and I watched it spin.

'So what are you doing here?' I asked, again.

She smiled and spread her hands in a shrug as she sprawled on my sofa. 'You know how these things happen to me.' She squelched out of her trainers and swung her feet onto the cushions. 'My room after the gig fell through. It was nearby, you might have heard about it.'

'I don't really go out now.'

'Do you still drink that rocket fuel?' she asked.

'Not much,' I said, but I was crossing to the freezer. 'And it's not—'

'Premium vodka, whatever, give me a glass.'

I poured some into mugs, the dingy white ones I bought right after you moved out. It was so cold it felt like it melted in the mouth, sublimating from ice into fire in the space between sips. She made a harsh noise at the first taste then went back for more.

'God, can you believe we finished a whole bottle of this once?'

'There were three of us then.'

'Still, it's poison.' She didn't slow down.

In the quiet between us, there was just the sound of the dryer and the beat of rain against the glass.

'We were younger, then,' she said, smiling down into her glass. 'Stupider.'

It was late. I was tired and I was drinking vodka and there was Moira, occupying her space on what had been yours and my sofa. It was where she played us her songs and cried over feckless girlfriends who left her for nice, stable women who owned dogs. She made us promise, once, never to get boring. I'd toasted to it.

'I'm sorry,' she said. 'For how it all went down.'

'Leave it,' I said.

'No,' she said, sitting up straighter, her voice too loud. 'We've never had this out and it's been long enough.'

'I don't want to hear it.'

'She felt terrible, she knew we blindsided you—'

'Don't.'

'—but I don't see why we can't all be grown-ups about it.'

'You've never been a grown up about a thing in your life.'

She froze as if she hadn't expected my participation in this conversation. I wanted to do something big and stupid like punch her but I breathed out hard through my nose and settled for putting my mug down on the table with a firm thunk.

'Would a grown up do this?' I asked. 'Turn up at someone's door in the middle of the night?'

'I told you, my room fell through,' she said.

'So you find another! You call a taxi. You don't go and get half drowned.'

'You always looked down on me. Not everyone is loaded.'

'You're exactly how I remember.'

'Well, you're nothing like I remember,' she said. 'There's no love here, none.'

And that was the problem. I had grown hard and sensible while she was still herself. We had both loved you, and both lost you, but she had survived it intact. I don't know how she did it.

'You don't give a shit about what I love,' I said, the word muffled.

She leaned back, comfortable. 'So you admit that you're still angry?'

'Of course I'm angry.' The vodka sat high in my stomach. I wished I was drunk enough to shout.

'Then why even let me in? You want to have it out.'

The dryer dinged, finished with its cycle.

'I'm going to sleep. If I'm lucky, you'll be gone by the time I wake up.'

'You should throw me out. You want to.'

'There's blankets under the coffee table.'

'But then you'd lose, wouldn't you?'

'Good night.'

I didn't sleep. I lay in bed, watching the rain run its rivers down the window. I thought about you and the last, terrible night. It was raining then, too. A determined drizzle. Your glove fell out of your bag onto the pavement, soaked through. I'd wanted you to stay and talk it out, but it wouldn't have done any good. We were both too stubborn. Moira was behind you, one of your bags over her shoulder. She'd looked so sad with her damp hair plastered to her head and it had made me so angry that she cried over a situation she created.

I almost missed her more, after. You had been a lover, a flurry of life and passion, but Moira was a conspirator, a sister in arms. She was the person who pushed me. You only ever waited for me, until you got sick of waiting.

You'd left a few things behind and I wanted to throw them after you and watch them be ruined. Instead, I got out a twenty litre box and filled it up with everything that reminded me of you. When you asked for it, later, I played dumb and you didn't push. I donated it all, unable to stomach throwing it away but too spiteful to give it back. I was always looking out for people wearing your things, after that.

I woke up early. The city is always clean, at least, after the rain washes out the smell of so many people living on top of each other, the dust and debris carried away. It was all freshness. Even the musty dampness of Moira's wet clothes had been carried away by the morning sun which shone through my window. The air had been moved aside in subtle ways.

She was knelt over in the fridge, the contents vomited onto the floor around her feet.

'Do you have bacon?' she asked.

'I'm a vegetarian,' I said, taking in the chaos.

'Eggs then?'

'I don't really like them,' I said. 'I usually skip breakfast.'

'What about pancakes?' She started going into the cupboard.

I took the ancient bag of flour from her and put it back. The corner was torn and left a trail of dust behind it. I wanted to look behind me and see that nothing had changed, that you were just late to breakfast wrapped up in your dressing gown, and I wanted not to have this anger filling me up, choking my heart. Moira watched me.

'Do you hear from her ever?' I asked.

'Now and then,' she said. She hoisted herself onto the worktop, not caring about the dusting of flour. 'It sounds like she's enjoying married life. They have a labradoodle.'

I nodded. I had heard about the wedding, but not from you.

'I wish we'd never met you,' I said. It was one of the things I'd always held onto, this wish, and never said out loud. Now it sounded like a lie.

Moira just smiled at me. 'If it hadn't been me, it would have been something else.'

'I'm calling you a taxi.'

'I'll walk.'

'Let me,' I said.

We sat by the window, waiting, watching the morning haze paint highlights on the rain-slick road. Years ago, all three of us would still be asleep. Moira would cook us breakfast while I kissed you awake.

The taxi arrived. I stopped her with a hand on her shoulder and pushed an umbrella into her hands. A cheap, collapsible thing I overpaid for in a chemist. It might just survive. 'Bring it back the next time you're in town.'

She smiled and she stepped out. She was a flash of warm shadow amidst the shining raindrops, lit through with cold crystal light. Everything gleamed, fresh and clean and new.

Jay G Ying

RECALLING

Part One, Apollo

R remains
silent

when I ask
Could there be any little joy
in our long war

in Yaffa
we let the blissed AC
broil our sweat

without
much philosophy

every bared chest
felt like a cut a single kiss
a betrayal

one pleasure deprived

the planets did
nothing
except split angels

of us

in the gold lighting
that club's tell
tale signs

the waves
only yesterday
beginning

their swallow of us

Part Two, Al-Ghaib

R enters first

always
the chance
to come through

as a carving

always
to find him outside
his body

by a gloriole
where the electric spirit
slumps to spit

I smell always the
poppies on his skin

on other men

and on our way out
the security
asked every miniature

of our new old lives
at the checkpoint
I say I remember

the evening too

well the dark tiles
flooded by his drink

foam from the corner
his arms split and
out of him pooled

that law of gravity

No one to hold my
things No blood to weigh
them to the floor

Part Three, Ishim

R's every action

twitch
or second sideways look

every yearn
of the buzz of a pocket
that holds a phone
in spasm at span's

length all of our time

I studied
I cross studied
I crossed again

that bouncer's wink
the long second
of the fingers by the bar

the parted
path its interrogation

I avoided looking
at him look
at the dancers

I knew in one way
already the beginning
of the end

in a paradox
I had foretold it
so in spite

it had come to pass

to be only a man
and then to be
just one more man

Part Four, Betheseda

R baptises

me mockingly
in the pools of troubled
waters two days later

I think back
to the pine trees by
the tanks of water each

reservoir green as
rotting meat turned
to water

I made myself

his hands first around
my neck then down
on my head

from which to water

I did not even fight him
nor resist like a law
made from water

unspoken
I recall surviving only
to see that orange

sun behind the water
like a glory

the forest of growing trees

I wanted

no food no
water no air no
sleep no rage no

desire no victor

but for him and his God

Laura Waddell

NONE OF SUMMER'S MY BUSINESS

The dogs are all screaming on hind legs
arrow taut accusing one another
and the teenagers are screaming too
out there in the dark behind hedges and cars

Thick heat filters through bus windows
Facing the sun on the city grid
One driver didn't wave to another yesterday
Maybe the glare was in his eyes

A fat bee commandeers the stairwell
squatting on the fourth stair up and what of it
You have to jump to get past from third to fifth
calves straining into being with a thud

There was a fire drill before lunch today
or maybe the heat just got to it
You were wearing a blue dress
Like the hottest part of the flame

None of summer's my business
but you turn away and into more of it
rummaging for figs to satisfy change of palate
flowers ripen and spritz soft air with pollen

I saw you wear sandals for the first time this year
but the next day was blustery
and you switched shoes again
summer is always on the move and I can't stop it

Eris Young

MEULES

Straw

The pilot's hands and knees burn with cuts. At least she is out of the water. Someone — a line of bristling someones — picks its way down the jagged slope as she looks up it. Despite a thrill of fear the pilot thinks first of Monet's Haystacks, of the one she saw with Ian at the National Gallery. *Meules*, the French word comes to her. It also means 'millstone'. Ian had taken pains that she pronounce it correctly. Made a little lesson out of it. She thinks of the straw packed around eleven bottles of Ardbeg, cradled in the sinking fuselage of her Percival Proctor.

The pilot — or perhaps just Margaret now, with the Proctor making its languorous journey to the bottom of the North Sea — is taken scratchily under the arms. The rain lashes them all. How can these haystack people be so sure-footed, black stick feet lost in the mudgloom beneath those massive straw cloaks? They try to make her walk but she cannot, so they drag her up the path. Her vision goes dark.

There comes a period — days? — of intermittent wakefulness, and intermittent pain. She's in a hard bed, scratchy blanket pulled to her chin. Drenched and shaking, she smells salt and algae and the inside of her own running nose. A stern-faced phantom sits beside her, holding a cup of something. The smell of it makes Margaret gag and she turns her face away. The phantom becomes Ian, looking on her with disapproval. He holds out the cup and she tries harder this time, struggling to make mouth and throat work in concert, but the broth won't stay down. A murmur of worried voices consult above her and she tries to wave them off. This state is not new to her. She's been through withdrawal before, and it will pass.

Candle

When she wakes properly, her sheets are dusty and smell of the sickbed, stale and bilious. A stout white candle sits on a side table under a window, next to her rescued kitbag. There's a clay cup and jug of water beside the bed which Margaret drains dry. She feels wrung out; her lips are in tatters. Her hands are steady. She's hungry.

It is either very early morning or dusk. Through a pane of wavy glass she can make out a fuzzy, lumpish horizon and her mental compass needle swings wildly. She's still wearing the clothes she wore when the Proctor went down. The kitbag, which she managed to grab before having to swim, held only keepsakes and small goods of little practical use. The carton of cigarettes, the packs of nylons, her purse and her mother's cigarette case have been set out in a row to dry. Someone has been through her things, Margaret realises with unease.

Her boots sit by the door and she pulls them on, stiff and crusty. Kitchen sounds come from further down the hall. She makes to follow them but catches a whiff of her own body. Down the hall, austere and cloistrous, she finds a stone-floored room. In one corner, a tap and zinc tub; in the other, a hole.

Coarse linen towels are stacked against one wall, and she finds a shaving kit and three wrapped bars of Ivory soap. She holds one in her hand, it's at once familiar and utterly foreign, lighter than air. She considers and abandons the idea of shaving her legs.

She crouches in the tub in two inches of frigid water, stripping away the fug of sicksweat. It's too chilly to wear wet clothes so she shakes out her shirt and trousers, still dry, to soften them where they have stiffened with sweat and salt water.

Dry and clothed, Margaret follows the sounds of a sporadic flow of women and girls, the oldest maybe seventy. Some are shorter and some are taller than Margaret, some plump, some bony to the point of androgyny, one or two of them pregnant. All except the oldest have the same florid complexion and pale brown hair, and the same kind of dark homespun dress or habit, belted with a braided cord.

She passes a doorway into a whitewashed room. It's missing a wall, open at the opposite end to a bright field of flower and heath. There are a number of girls here, facing the field in unmoving silence. Is this some kind of monastery?

The bustling kitchen is warm and welcoming after the abbeyish hallways. She's staggeringly hungry now. The stern-faced woman she remembers from her bedside presides, quietly directing the cooking of a meal and the laying of places at a massive scuffed table. The woman, a head shorter than Margaret but stout and hatchet-faced, pulls out a chair. The belt she wears is the prettiest thing about her, wide and elaborately knotted.

'You are feeling better, then?'

She speaks English with a Germanic accent that makes Margaret's gut clench. But she doesn't feel like a POW; no one has tried to restrict her movements, and anyway, she couldn't have blown all the way across the North Sea. Could she?

A bowl of porridge is set in front of Margaret, and kippers, and a lump of black bread. When the meal has been devoured a clay cup of tea is set down and Margaret snatches it. Proper English breakfast, ambrosia.

Where do they get all this? The tea, the soap. Is there no rationing? Perhaps, she wonders with a sliding sense of dislocation, she knows their supplier. Despite the apparent absence of men the people here don't have the harried, worn-down look they do back home. The woman sits.

'My name is Sigis.'

'Oh, pardon me, Margaret.' Sigis takes her hand in a surprisingly strong grip. 'What is this place, if you don't mind me asking?'

Sigis says something long and unpronounceable.

'What, er, country are we in?'

Sigis repeats the name. Should she ask for latitude and longitude? She has no map. Before she can think how to phrase her question, Sigis says, 'There is a war going on to the east, yes?'

Definitely not German, then. Margaret nods.

'We see the planes sometimes overhead. And you are fighting in it? You are a soldier?'

'Ah, no. Auxiliary air force,' Margaret hedges. 'Supply.'

'I see.' Sigis is inscrutable.

Margaret is certain now it was Sigis who went through her things, saw the cigarettes and the nylons and knew what they meant. Margaret comprehends, with a familiar dread, that she is entirely at this woman's mercy. She braces herself for a confrontation, but Sigis says, 'There will be a boat tomorrow to take you home.'

'A boat?'

'A mailboat. It will stop at an island not far from here and we will go to meet it. I will fetch you from your room at dawn. Until then, you may do as you wish, but I ask you not to disturb the acolytes in their work.'

Honey

Margaret is indeed left to her own devices. A little red-cheeked woolen girl comes in with a pail of milk and Margaret sidles out behind her. It's sunny, the clouds mountainous and fast-moving. The terrain reminds her of Mull, where she and Ian honeymooned, unable to afford anywhere farther from home. It was the most beautiful place she'd ever seen. She wandered off paths and clambered through thickets for a better view, the moments of peace as she waited for Ian to catch up. She remembers bracket fungus; a dead porpoise lying on a beach.

She descends a sloping path to the cliffside. She should find a village or something, some other people who might be more forthcoming about where she is. She'll walk the shore until she gets hungry, then turn back. At each tumbledown path to the sea she peers vainly at the rocks and surf for some sign of the Proctor, or perhaps a crate washed up, but she finds nothing. She passes a few cultivated fields, a couple of cliffside pastures, but these too are tended by the haystack women. Like the sheep, they sidle away at her approach.

She tries to see them the way Ian, the way Professor Ian Dumbarton, would see them. They are a bit primitive. The authority they afford Sigis, and her intricately woven belt, is conspicuous — matriarchal? She can't remember seeing any decoration or iconography, even the little chapel room had been bare inside. If Ian were here, he'd know what that meant. At the thought of Ian limping round this soaked and blasted place, squatting over a hole in the stone floor, she gives a single bark of laughter, and claps a hand over her mouth.

The seaside path takes her all the way around the island in just a few hours. She stands for a time, looking grimly up the path to the big house, then turns and makes her way inland. She follows a stream, drinking from it occasionally, the sun beating down on her. The stream deepens into a pool and she strips off to swim and rinse her clothing.

Basic training has been good to her body: she's shed the weight she gained carrying Rosie, and become lean, even muscular. She hasn't thought of Rosie in a long time, she realises with a pang. Losing her had been hard. For a fortnight afterwards, Ian had been relentless, reminding her doggedly of her failure. He'd hit her for the first time during that period.

When the war began it was almost a relief. Ian, a conscientious objector, had scorned her decision but he couldn't stop her enlisting, not when demand was so high. She remembers the desperation and loneliness of that time and her mind shies away from the thought, had the war not come, of what she would have done.

Things had been better for a while, then, but she couldn't avoid seeing Ian on leave days. Last time, they'd gone to the Ritz for lunch. She made an effort, put on makeup and the dress he'd bought her at Christmas. She decided she'd be sober for the whole thing. But after the easy camaraderie of the station, she'd felt ungainly and awkward in civvies. Ian had noticed as well,

'Look at you,' he said, 'hardly even a woman anymore.'

She'd been unable, in the end, to go without a drink. Remembering, she ducks her head under the freezing water, holding her breath until her lungs burn.

She lies on the prickling bank to dry off and falls asleep in the languorous sun. She wakes again as the wind picks her out in gooseflesh. The sight of a fading yellow bruise on her shoulder reminds her again how very far from home she is, and how soon she will be back there. For the first time since waking this morning she wants a drink.

She walks instead, aimless, leaving the stream behind. It's been worse, she can see that now, the last few months. It hasn't help that illicit booze has been such a lucrative sideline. She only got into the bloody business to have a bit of money Ian couldn't touch.

She crests a hill and finds a low cottage backed by a collection of tall beehives. She becomes aware of the familiar hum, as she descends the green slope, of little sunlit brown bodies swooping around her.

The keeper, in a veil and white smock over her woolen dress, sets the roof and crown board on the grass and lifts the top honey super tentatively, arms shaking. Before she can lose her grip Margaret has reached the foot of the path. She takes hold of the other corner of the super and together they lower it gently to the ground.

'Careful now,' says the keeper in a husky, mild voice.

Margaret helps her go through the bees. In companionable silence they trim off queen cups and check for brood. She is stung, once, on the left forearm. It's a clean, throbbing pain and Margaret is sorry to brush the creature's disemboweled body onto the grass.

They carry the honey super, divested of bees, into the little one-room cottage. The keeper is old, skinny and a bit frail, with a mane of unbraided silver hair. As she sits into a shaft of light at the rickety table in the cottage, the sun lights up a kindly, whiskery face.

'You are the one they pulled from the sea.'

'I think I climbed out, actually. I'm Margaret.'

'Thank you for your help, Margaret. I am Astrid.'

'My pleasure. My nan kept bees, though nothing as nice as your hives.'

They chat about the craft for a little while, about the funny habits of the little folk, as Astrid calls them. She is cheerfully evasive when Margaret tries to get more information about their location, but answers other questions.

'The girls here, they don't speak?'

'Why would they when you could not understand them?'

'You don't teach them English?'

'We don't teach them German, Faroe or Scots, either.'

Astrid stands, knees popping, and begins to bustle about. She is taller even than Margaret. The belt at her waist seems made of sunbursts, no — flowers, all wrought in cord. She offers Margaret a cup of tea.

'Or perhaps something stronger?'

She produces a bottle of something cloudy amber — mead? A stretching moment passes.

'Just tea please, thanks.'

Astrid pours herself a measure, and sets out a pot and teacup.

'Do you live here alone?' Margaret bites her lip, ready to apologise, but Astrid smiles indulgently.

'I do not share this house with anyone, if that is what you mean. But I would not say that I am alone.'

A silence settles which seems habitual for Astrid, then,

'Where are your men?'

'*My* men?'

'No, just, the men. If they're not at war, where are they?'

'I am afraid I don't understand your question. Have you not seen them out in the fields and in the house?'

'I—' Margaret subsides, frustrated, but doesn't want to antagonise this woman who has been so kind. She wishes Astrid would put the bottle away.

The sun is setting. This time tomorrow she will be on her way back to the mainland. How will she explain her failure to report to her SO? How will she explain her disappearance to Ian? She has most likely missed a leave day. Her gut clenches at the thought of what he will say, what he will do. If he's gone to the trouble of reporting her missing she will pay dearly for it when she returns.

The kitchen chair scrapes as Astrid pushes it back in. Margaret hadn't noticed her get up.

'I must go back to the big house for a while, but you are welcome to stay and finish the tea.'

She takes a straw cloak down from a hook and opens the door to the cottage. 'The wide path will lead you back when you are finished.'

Mead

The mead is very sweet. It makes her teeth sing. She drinks it in steady, businesslike swigs as she makes her way back to the big house under a full moon. Margaret knows the drink is making her maudlin but she lets the fantasy of a future here play out. She is an outsider but she could be useful to these woman. She can swing an axe and ply a hoe. She can help Astrid with her bees. She cast off wifehood to become a pilot. Could she do the same again, and become a woman who crafts and cooks and tends the earth? Could she discard the useless weight that is Margaret Dumbarton?

Soft sounds catch her attention as she makes her way from the kitchen to the little sickroom. She is passing the odd three-walled chapel. A shaft of moonlight spills from the door, slightly ajar. She kneels clumsily and puts her eye to the gap. The room is empty save for two people moving as one on the stone floor. A bright pair of heaving, pillowed breasts, a pair of downy legs wrapped fast around a narrow waist. The back above it is bony, ridges of spinal column revealing themselves anew with each thrust. The streaming light catches in a shining mane of silver hair. To one side is a heap of clothes; habits, straw cloak, stockings. Atop the discarded meule lies a belt of bright flowers. Margaret watches them for a time, entranced. Then, in a flash of clarity, she knows what she will do.

She finds the weird little water closet and crouches wobblingly over the hole. She will not miss this room. She gulps water from the tap. She pockets a bar of the Ivory soap.

Back in the sickroom, she shakes open the stiff, salt-rimed kitbag. The packs of cigarettes she went to such lengths to get are nothing but pulp, but the innermost may contain salvageable tobacco. The nylons too can be saved with a careful wash — they may indeed pay her way.

Her mother's cigarette case will need polishing; she tucks it into the left cup of her brassiere. The photo of Ian is slimy and unrecognisable, and she leaves it on the side table. Her passport and tags are mostly intact inside her leather purse but these too she discards, leaving them beside the photo. When she re-enlists it will not be as Margaret Dumbarton.

Alice Tarbuck

MARY GODWIN SHELLEY'S SECOND WIFE

exists as an error of punctuation, a crack
in the flow, a line read twice.
The second wife
walks through closed doors like a summer wind,
shivers like wet salad leaves, excises doubt
and undoes clothes like a pocket knife,
open at the blade.

Mary Godwin Shelley's second wife
nurses her unripe baby,
and holds her hands when it dies. Comes
to her when Claire and Shelley dance,
(for after all, a man may take three wives)
unfurls like a fern raised in deep shade
catches the air like orange blossom and scents
her collars with happiness, or plants.

Mary Godwin Shelley's second wife eats her out,
takes pleasure in it, buries her tongue and shouts
that women are intellect's true flame-keepers,
though her voice of course is muffled. Reads
tarot and cleans nothing, hangs like a bat
in abandoned churches, nibbles at velvet,
eats alabaster like pastilles, sighs aloud.

Mary Godwin Shelley's second wife
contains colour like a marble, climbs
in storms and licks white electricity
from trees. She sits on her haunches, curious,
while Mary Godwin Shelley weeps,
and puts a cold nose to her tear-stained face.
They laugh over tea on bright mornings,
and take off their stockings in rain.

Mary Godwin, Shelley's second wife,
never speaks on the subject.
Her wife, strong as stone,
invisible as spider's thread, plays the piano, hands
above the keys, winks over her shoulder,
stands in the rain with her hair loose, singing,
songs so very loud among the grave stones,
that they bring more life than a hundred
calcified poets' hearts.

Elva Hills

THE LANDSCAPER

East and Aldina lie on a naked mattress, filthy sheet strung across the window filtering dust. It's too hot to move, too hot to think, so they spend their days horizontally, deathly still.

Night is falling. While Aldina drifts in and out of sleep, East contemplates the hours of work ahead, when cool air finally blows through the sheet. It's illegal to take research out of the laboratory, but if the government hadn't given up the fight, suspending operations, she wouldn't have had to.

She peels her sweat-soaked body from the mattress. The heat is rising, surging.

Crackling.

She climbs over Aldina, soles burning as she crosses to the window, pulling the sheet aside. The horizon swirls black and orange, sparks dancing like fireflies amid a swarm of roiling black smoke.

'Aldina. Wake up.'

Her wife rouses, slowly at first, dragging her body to face East. Then her eyes open and she is the military officer again, springing from the bed.

East pads to her desk.

'Leave it,' Aldina says to her back. 'None of it matters now.'

She's right. About every textbook and notepad, computer and hard drive, except one. East topples piles of papers, sends nests of wires to the floor, until she finds it, fingers closing around hot plastic; the key.

A cough starts in the back of her throat. Through watering eyes, she watches Aldina sink a shirt into their jug. The water is pure, all they have left, but there will be no drinking it. The flames are coming.

Aldina reaches her first, pressing the damp cloth to her mouth and nose. 'We take these and we run.' Her hand is in East's, dragging her to the door, down narrows steps, pitch black in the coming storm. The fires of hell draw closer, air clogged with smoke. Dry from the endless drought, their apartment block is kindling to the flames. East can feel the fear of death in Aldina. It should be in East too, but her mind is on the key tucked in her shirts.

It could change everything. If it survives.

The world explodes, ground shaking, and East stumbles. Dust kisses her skin, a layer of gray over sweat. She follows Aldina's eyes to the ceiling. Two deep cracks snake across it, spreading. East's grip tightens, then she's running, holding Aldina's hand like a lifeline.

There are no windows in the jet. The last thing Sol saw before boarding at the foot of the sprawling metropolis, Casper, Wyoming, was the crop domes erupting like pellicles from an otherwise flat horizon.

Extraordinary things happen when you step into the dark and let yourself believe. That's what Sol's momma used to tell him when the power went out and they were left to eat their supper in pitch black. When the streets were alive with the sound of breaking glass and howling, to get him to quit his shaking. She wanted him to dream — dream his way out of that dump.

Maybe she'd have said something different if she knew twenty years later Sol would dream a path straight into the Red Zone.

The ship slopes to the ground. 'Almost home,' cheers the passenger beside him. Melville's foot hasn't stopped bouncing since take-off. Sol smiles, but the thought of getting off this jet terrifies him. *This will be my new home, this jet. There's nothing worth seeing outside.*

It turns, one side dipping, creeping closer to the ground; searching. When it finds a place to land, it balances, and Sol feels queasier than ever.

Melville places their hand on top of his. He looks at them; kind face, metal glinting on ears under a tangled bob of dyed white hair. 'We'll be alright.'

That won't last, Sol thinks. The hair or the sky-blue optimism. They're in the unknown; the dark. Sol doesn't know what to think or believe, but he's darn sure that won't last long at all.

East didn't like the presence of a military officer in her lab, no matter how much she enjoyed watching her fight with the vending machine each morning.

'This is a research laboratory. Remind me why I need military oversight.'

'The survival of this planet is a military issue. We are at war and we're losing.'

'War with who?'

Aldina was silent so long East thought she was ignoring her. 'Ourselves. Our mistakes.' She was standing over the screen — not authorised to touch anything in this lab, and yet East didn't stop her — flicking through charts of rising temperatures across the equator.

It started with the heat. Long periods of drought caused deadly dehydration. Crops failed, land burnt to a crisp. Floods destroyed half of Houston. The planet was transforming, like it no longer wanted them on it and was going into defence mode. Like a frightened armadillo, rolling up into a ball of hard shell.

The USA finally elected a president worthy of the role, who tore down it's walls, and evacuated everyone in the southern borders. But moving them was slow. In El Paso, those who could afford the journey without aid had already left. Those who couldn't were selected by a lottery. If your name was drawn, you and your family were relocated north.

Aldina proposed to East at the lab.

'You will never abandon your research. You're here to the end.' They were sharing a break on the roof, eyes on the shrivelled remains of a forest on the horizon as they passed a cold can of coffee between them. 'And I will never abandon you.'

Feet dragging on the desert scrub, East replays the memory in her head. There are people all around, each walking the same road, but East feels Aldina. There's a thread strung between their two hearts. She will never be lost.

'Your research might have saved us all.' Aldina catches up to her, her military march setting her at a faster pace than the rest, but her skin glistens with new sweat, cutting lines into the clay covering her skin. 'It's a shame the world will burn before you get the chance to finish it.'

East has finished it. The algorithm is untested, but why fear the risks when the world is already falling apart? Your existence erased?

'We have to get to the lab in Fort Worth. Last I heard, it's still standing. I can trigger it from there.'

Aldina places her hands on East's cheeks, fingers splaying behind her ears. 'We're heading north. If there's a place for us in this world, it's there. We have to survive.'

East shakes her head, pulling out of Aldina's soothing touch. If she lets herself think about all she's losing, she'll never go through with it. 'It's bigger than us. My place is here. You know that. You've always known.'

Aldina softens. 'And I said never.'

Sol still feels movement in his legs. Rising from his seat, he wobbles. Melville passes him a suit, turning their back to him. Sol has never had the privilege of modesty. He strips out of his clothes and pulls on the suit.

There are eight of them in total and they're all louder than Sol, fighting for spots in front of their exit. With a name like the Red Zone, it's no wonder people like Sol ended up in the

Earth-Recreation Facility. He imagines corpses, fires with a life of their own, floods strong enough to floor a city. Up until last year, the government didn't give a hoot about the Red Zone. Then it was all a flutter, and the Earth-Rec team was formed of members from the United Americas' top correctional facilities.

The door lets out a gushing sound and slides, giving way to a thin line of white light. Sol runs his hands over the seal of his helmet. Beside him, Melville laughs, their painted lips split in a grin so wide Sol can see their overlapping teeth.

The light spreads, rushing into the cabin. Sol shields his eyes. The jet's voice floods through his helmet and everyone falls quiet, listening to their warden. 'Oxygen depleted in 120 minutes.'

Without a dome over their heads, the air will be hot enough to burn their lungs from the inside out. You'd be better off drinking gasoline than failing to get back to the ship in time.

'Sol.' Meville's eyes appear wider through their helmet. 'You with me?' They hold out their hand for a shaken agreement.

Sol stares at the other inmate. He had them pegged as older, late twenties, but their excitement rewinds the years. Sol feels tired by comparison. Worn down. Used to flying solo and stuck in his ways. This is another journey he planned to make alone.

But not all plans are worth keeping. Sometimes you have to step into the dark and unknown. To believe in something bigger than your fears.

He takes their hand.

Truth weighs on her shoulders, making every step harder: *we are going to die*. Aldina knows it too; East can see it in the sad tilt of her smile, her hand taking East's like they're children lost in a forest.

The air is toxic, scorched earth under their feet still smoking. East feels the heat through her shoes, rubber turning sticky — melting.

'You really think it will work?'

'I'd be a poor scientist if I didn't question my own research.' It isn't the answer Aldina wants. East stops, hands on knees. Winded, every breath raw. What she would give to be back in her clean lab, fresh oxygen streaming through the aircon. 'But I would have left it to burn in our apartment if I thought it wouldn't work.'

Not a fool's hope. Their last hope. They were reaching the end of their story, and all they had left was this wish upon an eyelash that East's work hadn't been for nothing.

Maybe their lives were never supposed to change. Their generation wasn't supposed to know any different. Asking people to give a shit, it was too much. They'd pushed their luck. But it could be better for the people of tomorrow, if they fought this battle today. East didn't have to see the change to believe in it.

Two weeks walking. Two weeks crunching bugs and sucking on the innards of charred cacti for sustenance. When they arrive at Fort Worth, the city is a crumbling ghost town. Their search for food proves a waste. Every supermarket, 7-Eleven, every cupboard in every house picked clean.

The thought is heavier: *we are going to die before we even get there.*

The specimen is fragile. Sol can tell just by looking at it, petals like purple rays bursting from an orange sun. He aches to take off his glove as he cradles the soil held together by it's net of roots, reddish-brown crumbling through his fingers. What was it Warden said? Contamination from organisms may result in injury or death.

He slides it into the pod, twisting it shut and activating the filter. The specimen will remain in this pod during shipment back to Casper, until tests are run and it's proved clear of toxicity.

Sol checks the monitor on his wrist. The timer rolls past 14:00.

Shit. 'Mel, we gotta go.'

Twenty minutes out, giving them eighty minutes to collect material, then twenty minutes to walk back. His knee cracks as he pushes off the ground.

'Mel?'

He turns toward the cluster of small plants bordering the meadow, covered in bulbous red fruits. Last he looked, Melville was sitting cross-legged in the middle, logging their comments on a private stream.

God, Mel. Where did you go?

His heart races, guzzling his oxygen. If audio is malfunctioning, Melville could be back at the ship, waiting for Sol with a tin mug of powdered coffee. A glint of light catches Sol's eye some five strides ahead, raw sunlight shining off the glass orb of a helmet.

Mel.

Sol drops to the ground at their side. They're asleep, or unconscious, their body limp as he shakes them. Eyelids flutter. Sol's oxygen is thin, but a glance at Mel's monitor tells him theirs is spent.

Sol searches their body, eyes scouring the surface of their suit. There must be a breach, a hole or puncture.

'Come on, Mel, don't make me leave without you.'

Even as he says it, he knows it'll never happen. He knew the risks signing up; knew they were sent here to clear up space in the facilities. To the big shots back in Casper, people like him and Melville are nothing but collateral.

Sol touches the seal on his helmet — standing on the edge of darkness, bracing for the leap. Rips it from his head. His chest ignites, seconds from bursting. Sol grabs the fabric of his suit. It's hot and the suit is no use to him now. Pulls it down over his shoulders so he's bare but for his vest. He takes a deep breathe, inhaling the toxins, the poison. But the air is sweet. Like blossom tea and honey, calming the storm in his chest.

No more burning.

No burning at all.

Mel's lips, the same ones to kiss him a week after landing, are turning blue. Sol takes their helmet in his hands, pressing forehead to the glass. If this is a mistake...

Mel is dead either way.

Gently, he eases the helmet from Mel's head, careful not to tug the white hair, black at the roots.

He rubs their lips, feeling for breath, fingers working their way to their neck, searching for a pulse.

Mel gasps with their whole body.

Relief pours over Sol like a waterfall.

Aldina heads up the stairs, letting the banister hold the bulk of her weight. 'You find the computer. I'll search for supplies.'

East pats her chest, untucking the key. Everything she wears is damp with sweat, her hair heavy and lank with grease as she smooths it out of her face. Not long now, then she can sleep.

Power is out across Fort Worth, but no government would build a research laboratory without backup generators. Warm yellow light spills over the lab as East pushes the door open. It's a chaos of discarded equipment and records, cockroaches skittering around the debris.

The key is a slender plate of hard plastic, copper and gold labyrinth threaded across its face. East slides it into the override, Aldina's feet heavy on the stairs.

Too fast. East braces herself to run when something soft thumps against her chest.

'Honey buns.' Aldina holds one up, before ripping open the packaging and stuffing it into her mouth. Sticky pastry covers her cracked lips.

East devours her own in two bites, pain shooting in her stomach in anticipation. As she types, the screen flickers, white to black. She has written and re-written this code a thousand times. It's printed into her memory. She's waited so long to do this; to change the world.

Vessels lie in wait between Fort Worth and El Paso; one

command and they'll activate.

'How long will it take?'

East resents the question. Aldina already knows the answer. East doesn't need to say it aloud. They'll be long dead before the first signs of change appear, and buds open before a new sky.

East holds her finger over Enter, eyes finding Aldina. She has organised the whole room like she's preparing for an inspection, cupboards emptied, contents arranged according to purpose.

East presses the key. 'It's done.' Her words sound how they feel — like breaking. 'I suppose we should get comfortable.'

Aldina's eyebrows shoot up, breaking her mask of flaking dirt. 'What are you talking about, *dulzura de mi vida?* We're not done yet.'

'Look at us. We're covered in blisters.' She thrusts out her arms. 'We're going to die out there. We're starving, Aldina.' She sounds like a petulant child. She hasn't drunk enough water to cry, but grief forms sharp shards in her chest. 'A honey bun isn't going to cut it.'

'We'll find something else on the road north.' Aldina forgets her inventory and spins East's chair so they're facing each other. East can feel the cracks on Aldina's lips as she presses them to her forehead. She smells like sugary, salty cinnamon.

'It's impossible.'

'Extraordinary things happen when you let yourself believe. Beautiful and impossible things.'

Sol looks around the circle of inmates, faces transforming with the fire. They are past Warden's sensor range, stripped out of their suits. A message will reach Casper that they're MIA, presumed dead. Perhaps another team will be sent in their place, but that's an ordeal for tomorrow. Tonight, it's enough just to live.

The clearing is a far cry from the cell Sol shared with five others. He can stretch his arms over his head, lie back and look upon the stars, not the mouldering base of the next bunk up, nor the grey film of the dome.

His belly is full with fruits of the likes he's never seen before, let alone sampled. Laughter swells as a younger inmate across the fire lets out a ground-shaking belch. Sol wrinkles his nose, but he's happy — so happy he laughs with them.

'Room for one more?'

Sol holds out his arm. Mel nestles their head onto his shoulder, as if there isn't an entire world open to them.

It's a feeling Sol has never experienced before, that he could do anything, be anything, not a criminal but a hero of his own story, not hungry and hollowed out but full to bursting and eager to see tomorrow.

'I don't want to fall asleep.' Curling his arm, he reels them in, kissing the dark roots of their hair. 'What if I wake up and it's all a dream?'

They sit up enough to kiss his lips, their stubble rough on his chin. Their voice is thick with drowsiness. 'Then it's a dream worth holding out for.'

Rachel Plummer

IRIS, THE OLDEST PARTICLE PHYSICIST AT CERN

In one direction, she releases an albatross.
In the other, a vulture.
They plunge through the pipes like light.

Here, the wing meets no resistance
to its lust for acceleration.
Momentum is angular.

Deep underground Iris leans on the laws
she's defying. Her bones
are hollowing,

small tunnels in the dark
where the God of Almost-Nothing could crack
his soft shell open.

The circle floods with flight.
The miles-wide circle with its cargo of feathers.
The birds collide

head-on, and split
into a flock of gannets, hungry, crying
out at the shock of existence.

Iris weeps.
There's nothing like speed
to reveal what you're made of,

she says, but finds speech
falling from her like gravity.
Strange. She spreads herself wide as a wing.

She's itching to rise.
She's made for collision.
Iris bursts through the Earth like a song.

TITAN ARUM

I tuck myself under the spathe
as if it were my mother's pleated skirt.
Corpse-flower. Corpse-stiff and sweet,
the rotted grunt of its scent
enfolding me like a red womb,
holding me tight, safe against the spadix.

Cock-flower, they called it. Misshapen.
But they were men, stumbling
through Sumatra with their big knives
and their Latin. I can't help but call it
clitoral, raw and unfolding, damp
as that intimate skin exposed.

I press my nose closer into the rot,
think of how I held the hardening body
of a rabbit in my hands once
until it ripened like this flower.
Unmistakable. The smell
of cells undoing themselves like bows.

I let it swallow me down to its core,
strange pollen, I sink into the swollen
shaft, my fingers turn to root, my eyes,
I drown in hothouse soil. Consumed.
Outside, flies drip down the windows
and the earth is ripe with petrichor.

NIMBLEMEN

For us, the night sky
is a dancefloor. Look at us ceilidh
under the disco ball moon.

Fabulous warriors. Merry
dancers. Bonny lads in green
lipstick, flicking

our well-glittered hair.
Even the air is dancing tonight,
it splits the willow,

it knows all the moves.
Tonight if you're lucky
you'll look up and spy us

dancing round our handbags
until we're sweating
blood, drop by drop

onto the rock below.
Heliotrope. Our beautiful
red-flecked jade.

For us, the night sky
is a discotheque thrumming
with neon.

Just look at those lights,
the strobe of us strutting our stuff
until dawn.

SELKIE

The secret me is a boy.

He takes girlness off like a sealskin:
something that never sat right on his shoulders.

The secret me is broad-shouldered;
the sea can't contain him,

the land can't anchor his waves
to its sand.

The secret me swims
with the big fish, brash, he swaggers

like a mermaid, bares teeth
like daggers, barks at the moon when it's thin.

He's whiskered, that boy. Thick-skinned.
Quick-finned, always turning tail.

He wears his own skin like a sail,
lets it carry him to where

salt swallows mouthfuls of air.
Let them find me there by the shore:

the girl-seal with a secret
boy inside. Rough-voiced. Black-eyed.

Washed bare
as the beach by the tide.

Heather Parry

MR. FOX

Caleb moved to a new town when he was seventeen years old, which is about the worst time of your life to move to a new town. Caleb's mother had died, and in their home city there was too much of her; she was in every gallery, every theatre, every vintage clothing store that she'd loved. To Caleb these visions of her were comforting, but to his father they were vicious. Caleb's father grew tinier and tinier under the weight of his grief, until the city seemed too vast and feral. The new town was small, ever so small, and lots of the buildings there had wood against the windows, but it was empty of their mother. The houses there were on sale for one or two pounds each, so Caleb's father sold their city flat, paid off their debts, and had some money left to turn the house they'd purchased into a home. All that Caleb had of his mother were her furs.

Caleb had one year left of college so he was enrolled at a grey, brutalist sixth form. On his first day, wanting his mother's warmth, he threw one of her red furs on over his raincoat and walked to school. The fractured groups in his year all turned as he entered the gates and padded up to the front steps. They watched him, sneering and giggling, until someone threw a rock and he ran into the building. In the corridor, a boy tried to tear the coat from his back, so Caleb ran to the bathroom and bundled the fur into his rucksack, stroking it as if it were alive. For the rest of the day, he was teased and called names. The next morning, Caleb left his mother's furs safely stored in his wardrobe, and set off from home, saying goodbye to his father. But instead of going to college, he spent the day wandering through the small streets, looking at the quiet people in their quiet homes. If he was to be lonely, then he would be alone.

The town was a clockwork toy set, with its identikit terraces and its grey-brown brick. The colours were scratched off the playgrounds, with only charcoal-coloured metal left. It was all angles and jagged edges, with clockwork people going from work to home and home to work, all at the same time, moving in lines. On Saturday mornings they went to the library, on Sunday evenings they went to the pub, and on bank holidays they packed their small brown suitcases and took the grey train to the coast. Caleb's father was always amongst them, keeping his face to the floor and shuffling along with few words.

Yet there was a man in the town that was unlike the others. The man was red-haired and freckled on the face, with a thick square jaw and shoulders so large they left him no neck. He wore workman's boots, old Levi's jeans, an array of jumpers with holes at the elbow, and always, always an orange-red fur stole. He lived on the outskirts of town, in a flat one flight of stairs down from the road, behind an orange-red front door that had black paper taped over the windows. Caleb started to watch this man every day, heading straight to his street in the morning and following him wherever he went.

The man always left his house in the late morning, his eyes half opened, blinking rapidly. He kept to the shadows as long as he could, the stole around his shoulders never quite settled but never quite falling off. He went to the butcher's daily, the post office sometimes, the greengrocer's once a week, but never to the pub, or the library or to the coast. He never spoke a word to anyone else, and if asked any questions, he folded in on himself and scurried home.

He never left in the afternoons or the evenings, as far as Caleb could tell, though Caleb had to be home before dinner so his father wouldn't become suspicious. The man must have been an early riser, though, because no matter what time of the morning Caleb made it to his spying-place, the doorstep milk had always been taken in.

The man did washing on a Wednesday, hanging out his clothes on a line at the bottom of the stairs. But never, Caleb noticed, did he wash the fur stole.

The end of college came, with little complaint from Caleb's father about his lack of qualifications and little complaint from his teachers that he did not sit exams. The greyness was seeping into their household and draining Caleb's father of all his colour. Caleb worried that it was affecting him too. He got an afternoon job and moved into a one-pound flat of his own, two flights of stairs up, behind a blue door with no glass on it at all, just three streets away from where the man lived. He took his mother's furs with him. He settled into a new routine, getting up early no matter the season, leaving his house every morning at the appropriate time, and watching the man go about his daily rounds.

One day, as winter came around and the mornings grew colder, Caleb combed his hair neatly and put on his raincoat. He set off from home and headed straight to the butcher's. He arrived fifteen minutes before the man was scheduled to arrive, and he anxiously waited outside, playing with his cuffs. As the man finally turned the corner, Caleb darted inside and stood staring at the prime beefs and pig's knuckles. As the man slid in beside him, Caleb did his best not to stare.

The butcher nodded at his fur-swaddled customer, going into the back to retrieve a pre-placed order. The man stood by the glass-covered counter, his feet twitching, and Caleb could have sworn that the stole was moving, loosening and tightening itself around the man's upper arms and wide back. There was no breeze inside the shop but the fur was moving, bristling against bicep and chest. Despite himself, Caleb glanced up at the man and couldn't turn away. The man felt Caleb's gaze and moved further from him. The butcher returned with a paper-wrapped item, or rather, two items, their unskinned legs and dangling paws visible just beneath the edge of the paper, their long ears just visible above. The man slid two uncrumpled fives across the counter, took the parcel underneath his fur, and left.

The next day, Caleb went to the butcher's again at the same time, leaping inside as the man arrived. This time, he waited until the butcher went to fetch the rabbits, then turned to the man. He said something about the tougher meat that time of year, the smaller animals. He mentioned his own taste for the tender flesh of rabbits, stewed or barbequed. How many people wouldn't eat them, through superstition or sensitivity. The man neither responded nor ignored, but was clearly spooked by the attention. He simply stared forwards, gently trembling, and when his meat came and he paid his money, he ran out of the shop.

The man did not return to the butcher's shop. Caleb assumed that his orders would be delivered from then on, and he was right.

The man stopped going out in the mornings. Caleb quit his job in the afternoons to watch over the man's house, but he didn't appear then either. After a week, Caleb went home, to his grey things behind his blue door, and he took his mother's furs out of the wardrobe and wore them all at once. But still Caleb felt scooped out, bereft. He was missing the warmth he'd started to get from knowing that the man was there. He put the furs away and went out and spoke to people in the town, bringing the conversation around to the burly man in the orange-red fur stole, but none had seen him nor cared to speak of him. It was a bleak and cold winter in that small town, and Caleb felt more alone than ever.

It turned January. Taking sandwiches, flasks of Ovaltine and all the blankets he could carry, Caleb set up a den for himself in the bushes across from the man's door, hiding down in the ochre, the dead leaves, the frozen soil. He ate and drank through cracking lips, wishing for a stole of his own. As night fell, he squinted, adjusting his eyes to the dark, barely daring to blink for what he might miss.

It was after two when the man appeared. The door opened just a few inches and the man stepped out. He moved quickly, sprinting up the one set of stairs and down the road. Caleb threw off his coverings and followed behind in the blackness, close enough to see, but far enough to stay undetected.

They turned one corner, then the next, then the next. The man struggled to stay silent, letting out a yap here and there, an odd sort of barking. Suddenly he tripped, fell — no. He dropped to all fours and he began to run, perfectly balanced, quicker than Caleb could keep up with. The man's stole slipped from his neck and, suspended in the air, it followed behind him, resplendent and full and tipped with pure white. The man took off into the night and Caleb couldn't hope to follow.

Caleb was back in his bush-den when the man returned, his barking quieted, his gait once again human. In his fists were bleeding creatures, rats and such like, the fur stole safely back where it belonged, around his neck. Caleb sniffed a droplet of snot back into his nose and the man whipped his head in Caleb's direction. Nestled as he was and wrapped in darkness, Caleb was sure he couldn't be seen. Yet the man's gaze held on him for minutes. He slowly, quietly, went down his one set of stairs and behind the orange-red door. Caleb stayed there until he was sure he wouldn't be seen again, then gathered his things and bolted for home.

Caleb stopped watching the door. He started making visits to his father, who was greyer and more opaque by the day, and asked the older man to show him how to sew. The old man brightened slightly, his cheeks flushing pink. For hours each day, Caleb sat at the sewing machine with his father, watching how his hands worked, how the needle went into the material and fixed everything together. Caleb went to the library, taking and returning book after book from the nature section. He started visiting the butcher, and taking cuts of meat he'd never bought before. Finally, Caleb opened up this wardrobe and took out his mother's furs.

Three months passed by. Caleb was ready.

He choose a night in March, the first fair night of the season. He took the piece that he'd worked so hard on and stepped into it. He pulled up the patchwork fur outfit around his legs and over his bottom. He wrestled his arms into the arms of the costume, feeling the scratch of the underside of material against his skin. He'd sewed a zip into the front of the one-piece, so he could close it easily from the crotch to the neck. He flipped the hood over his head. The fur around Caleb was not a steady red, but ranged from yellow to grey to brown to white, with flecks of orange where he could find them. The funk of old clothes was constant, but inescapable. Alongside the smell of dust and darkness was the smell of his mother.

Caleb rubbed the outfit against himself, felt the warmth it brought. He turned around; it was a snug fit, but it suited him. From his buttocks hung a weight, an old stole that had been repurposed, but one that did not float in Peter's wake. Some things just cannot be faked.

Caleb closed his blue door behind him and set out into the night, warm and swaddled and bathed in cold sweat. He turned the three corners to the man's street and stared down the one set of stairs. He stopped. The outfit would not be enough.

An hour later. Caleb stood at the top of the stairs, breath heaving, the fur stuck to his skin with perspiration and dripping blood. His cheeks were red, his teeth bared to show what was trapped between. He held his tongue back in his mouth, so as not to rub against the damp skin of the rats, and held back a retch whenever their two tails scratched his neck. He stepped to the orange-red door and knocked firmly. The black paper was peeled back. A pause. The door opened.

The man looked at Caleb. He took in his mottled pelt, the costume of a feral creature, the colour it brought. He took in the bouquet of two dead rodents between Caleb's teeth, their blood running down Caleb's chin, his lips drawn back in an unnatural snarl. He took in the wild eyes above the creatures, the way they looked at him. Caleb said nothing, but continued to pant, standing in front of the man, asking for nothing but asking for everything.

The man pulled his lips back, tilted his head and pressed his face into Caleb's. He took one of the rats in his own mouth, let the blood flow over his chin and onto his neck. The man's lips brushed Caleb's. Caleb felt his balance topple. The man took Caleb's hand and led him inside, and as he did so, the man's tail fell from its hiding place around his shoulders, and followed behind him, tickling the floor.

Jonathan Bay

DEAR CHRISTOPHER

I was wrong to not buy you four hamburgers
when you were fourteen. I did not understand
the depth of your hunger. I do not think
I can blame it on the searing heat, or the steep descent
from the mountains, or the bleary traffic.
I thought having *that* many hamburgers was an
extravagance
like bills in your wallet only the bank can break, shampoo
purchased on a trip and left unfinished, even
the audacity of fronted money.
I now know the torrent of testosterone hunger.
Water in a desert — to it is four hamburgers,
three fries, a shake and bottomless coke, and still more.
It is animal, meaty, void-like — but forever. It is that melancholy tone
you put me through for two hours, the songs
you raged at me from the back seat of the minivan.

FREE NIPPLE GRAFT TECHNIQUE

Unlike flowers, cut nerves
never blossom. They misfire
in the vessel of my body
and smoke my pectorals.
I feel their sizzle in a deep breath
or the burning imprint of a palm.

It was the flick of the scalpel's smile
that flayed them, ribboned
the gentle threads — excised the whole
nipple, the colour of pursed lips.
A poppy planted back
on my chest, smaller, deflated. Never again
a visual presence in the cold.
Flat as a stamp licked and pressed
to the body with determination.
Nothing like the surgeon's cartoon.

Zoe Storrie

CONTINENTAL DRIFT

It's mid January, but on the bus journey from the airport to the hotel, everything we pass looks like Christmas. The driver tells us that many people keep their holiday lights up longer until the daylight stretches further. He tells us that the sun set before 4pm today. I count the rows of lights and gleaming orange windows as we make our way in to the city, trying to imagine what it must be like to adjust to this — so much darkness and then gradually, midnight sun.

I didn't want to come on the trip. Nel had come flying in from work just before Christmas, shouting that she'd found the perfect gift. Her boss, Brian, had booked a holiday to Reykjavik for him and his wife, but now he had a slipped disc and they couldn't go. She'd spoken so fast it had felt like watching a badly dubbed film. 'It wasn't difficult to change the names on the bookings,' she said breathlessly, 'everything is sorted — flights, transfers, accommodation, even trips!' She'd bristled when I'd reminded her that just the day before she'd been complaining about the cold in Glasgow, telling her that in Iceland, the snow might be up to her bellybutton. I was missing the point, she'd said. We could reconnect. We might see some whales, the northern lights. It was an adventure, the kind we'd stopped having. And if it was the flight I was worried about, she'd already booked me an appointment with the good doctor who would be sure to give me some diazepam. I looked at her hard, her flushed cheeks and giddy energy, and told her I'd go up to the loft and look out our old ski suits.

When we wake up on our first morning, it's still dark. We're going downstairs to the hotel's continental breakfast, and then on to the Blue Lagoon.

'I wish Brian had given us the first day off, to get our bearings in the city,' I said.

'The city's small, we can do it tonight after dinner,' Nel said into her coffee.

'It'll be dark again then.'

'Heather, shut up,' she says, and she leans in to me, kissing me with a mouthful of butter and jam.

On the bus, the driver tells us that we're wasting our money, that we would've been better visiting an entirely natural spring. We smile and thank him, promising there'll be a next time.

The land around the lagoon is beautiful. We're told it's a lava field, like the volcanic surface of another planet. Ahead, I see rising steam and overspills of the milky blue water near the entrance. We are given a wristband and are told that we must shower before entering the water. A sign tells us to remove our costumes. In the locker room, women remove their clothes unselfconsciously. Nel barrels our bags in to the lockers and starts to do the same. I feel a surprising panic, and then a sharp embarrassment about this strange cultural prudishness I didn't know I had. There's a more sinister feeling too, pushed down deep in my gut. I'm thinking of PE changing rooms at school, of girls shrieking if I looked at them, creating human shields for each other while they took off their school skirts. Nel tugs at my jacket and when I look back at her, she's naked, swim suit in hand.

'Hurry up, come on, nobody is looking!'

I sit on a bench and fold myself small, limbs all at odd angles seeking maximum protection. I peel everything off slowly and stuff them in to the locker. I feel the familiar currents of anxiety shooting down my arms, like pins and needles but softer, somehow. Nel sticks out her hand, and I follow her to the showers, almost pressed against her back. We wash quickly. I keep my eyes on my wife. Her hair is tied up and I find a scar on the nape of her neck that looks pink enough to be new. I wonder what happened. I look at the constellation of moles on her back that I've traced for half of our lives.

The first time I took Nel to visit the village I grew up in, she constantly wanted me to stop the car on the drive there so that she could take pictures of the valleys, the sprawling mauve flowers; my namesake. When I got impatient she said to me, 'You're just so used to this that you take it for granted, take a second to appreciate it.'

I blink hard and try to cough down the thickening in my throat, splash my face with water so that it's already wet. We put our suits on and walk in to the teeth of the cold.

We submerge ourselves, desperate for heat. It's like a perfectly drawn bath. I can't see our bodies through the chalky water and it feels nice to navigate through feeling. We scoop handfuls of silica mud from crates in the rock along the pool's edge and smear it on our faces — the tourist guide had promised rejuvenation. The steam from the water meets the grey of the sky and it feels like wading through a prehistoric fog. Before long, it starts to snow. The flakes melt as soon as they hit the water, but gather on our muddy faces, in our hair. I laugh at Nel then — flaky face mask, snowy head, the way she keeps scrunching her eyes up and glaring at the stag party behind us, splashing around with a Go Pro and plastic pints of beer. I squeeze her hand under the surface, feeling the crinkled ridges in her fingers. She holds on tight, and as the snow slows and the sky blues, I feel a surge of gratefulness for slipped discs. That night, in the hotel room, we love each other like teenagers.

Day two takes us on the Golden Circle Tour. A journey out of the city to visit a geothermal area with shooting geysers, Gullfoss waterfall — one of the most famous in the country — and Thingvellir National Park, where they have filmed some scenes for *Game of Thrones*. Our tour guide is astounding, switching seamlessly between five languages. She tells us stories about the white land we trundle over, as a blizzard obscures our view. She speaks of Huldufolk, hidden people, or elves that live among the rocks. She tells us that they are more than a story for children, and that she knows of a family denied planning permission for their home because they wanted to build on Huldufolk land.

Our first stop is a surprise, something we must have skimmed over in the leaflets. The bus pulls in to a car park and immediately we are all illuminated by gold light. As we step from the bus, I see rows of glowing greenhouses. Birta, our tour guide, tells us that geothermal heat is used to grow tomatoes all year round. We are taken inside and shown the produce. The tomatoes are fat, bulbous, resplendent. The golden light makes them look biblical. We each have a glass of tomato soup and it is delicious in a rich way that makes me feel warm. 'Better than your mother's,' I say to Nel, who acts shocked and then agrees, swearing me to secrecy. We leave with a bag full of tomato based produce: chutney, jam, chicken rub, even a dessert sauce.

I wake up with my face pressed against the window and a finger in my ribs.

'Why did you insist on the window seat if you're not even going to look?' Nel whispers, trying to take pictures of something beyond my head.

I rub my eyes and apologise, offer to swap sides.

She shakes her head no. 'It's too late.'

This time when we exit the bus, the wind chill gnaws at my hands like an animal. It slithers up my sleeves, aiming straight for the bone. I tie the cuffs of my jacket as tight as I can and pull my snood over my mouth and nose. A crowd has gathered in a circle. We make our way towards them just as it happens. Strokkur, the geyser we have come to see, erupts, shooting a fountain of water 20 meters in to the sky. The crowd gasps and claps, camera shutters clicking as they catch the spray. Nel is smiling now, recovering from her mood on the bus.

We explore the area while we wait for another eruption.

The ground has been dyed by sulphur and copper, the grass around the geysers the colour of egg yolk. We laugh at a sign warning visitors not to touch the streams of hot water, as they can reach 100 degrees. I wonder if anyone has tried it anyway, not accepting the caution until they can feel the pain in their own body. Birta approaches us to tell us that the geyser is due to erupt again soon. We join the circle and wait. The water begins to bubble and pool. It rises, first like a great blue blister, then breaks free and blasts skyward. The sun catches the spray in the right way and a small, fleeting rainbow forms. I try to formulate a joke that doesn't come.

Gullfoss, the waterfall, is only a short drive away. From where the bus drops us, it appears as if the river is swallowed by the earth. We follow the path towards the roar of the falls as it slowly comes in to view. The water rushes through its valley in stages, as if tumbling down a staircase. The path is narrow and slick with ice, but we edge forward, moving as close as possible to the thundering mouth. Parts of the waterfall are frozen. The ice gathers in thick, snow brushed clumps, on top of one another like molluscs. I think of the surface of the moon: crater crusts, molten mountains.

'It reminds me of Pompeii,' Nel says, showing me a zoomed in image on her camera of alien-like moulds of glittered ice. 'There could be people in there.'

We have lunch and head to our final stop before the sun goes down. Birta tells us about the geography of the national park as the bus takes to the road again. She tells us that we are about to walk between the North American and Eurasian tectonic plates.

'Our country,' she says, proudly, 'is the only place in the world where you will get to experience this, to touch this, above sea level. It's very interesting that Iceland exists at all, actually. But here we are.'

The rift valley is surrounded by majestic, volcanic cliffs. The lava fields are covered in grass, the green visible through thinner patches of snow. To see this against the dramatic fissures in the rock, to experience the dark, space-like geology, makes me understand the Icelandic belief in Huldufolk. The sky is darkening and the surroundings feel even more mythological as we meander along the trail. The snow returns in a slow, soft drift. I think of the night still to come, of the wide bathtub in the hotel, the unopened wine. I try to catch Nel's eye but she's somewhere else.

We have a browse through the visitor's centre when we reach the end of the trail. I pick up a mug with a watercolour impression of the waterfall etched across it.

'I'm getting this for my mum,' I tell Nell, her head disappearing in to an Icelandic wool jumper. It takes longer than it should for her to reappear and I know that she will be making a face behind the thick knit. Mum only moved out in September, after being with us for almost a year. She came to us in the early stages of dementia. By the time I agreed to put her in a home, she thought she was still a school teacher and would complain about the amount of books she had to mark. Before it got so bad, when she still knew me, she would often ask if I'd met a nice man yet. Nel insisted that it was deliberate; she said it only ever happened when she was in the room. 'She's got a glint in her eye, she knows fine well who I am' she said. After a while Nel had stopped having her tea with us and started bookmarking local care facilities on my laptop. The day we came home without her, I felt like I imagined a parent would when their kids move out. We sat on the couch and tried to remember how to be together.

Our final two days are slow. We have coffee in the city, come away from the flea market with other peoples' junk, admire the colourful buildings and surrounding mountains from Hallgrimskirkja's observation tower. We hide from the pelt of hailstones in Harpa concert hall, watching the sea through the geometric panes of coloured glass. Pink seafoam, yellow clouds, orange oystercatchers. In the gift shop Nel buys an ornament of a troll and doesn't laugh when I ask if that is her gift to her mother.

On our last evening, we skip the hotel meal and go in to the city for dinner. I choose the restaurant based on TripAdvisor reviews and the promise of variety. The interior is cosy with low ceilings and glass table lanterns. We order some local beer, a pitch-black, smoky bottle that tasted a bit like chocolate. Nel closes her menu. 'What are you thinking of ordering?' she asks.

'The burger, I think.'

'Do you not think you should try a local dish? Doesn't that make it feel more authentic? We have burgers once a week, at least.'

'Nel, you know I wouldn't like it. It'd be a waste of money, and it's hardly cheap. I picked here so we could both be happy.'

'But you won't even try.'

'I know what I want.'

'Me too,' she said, excusing herself to the bathroom.

My burger is delicious. Nel eats her choice slowly, a type of whale meat with potatoes. I feel uneasy as I watch her cut the pink meat into small cubes and chew until her jaw looks slack. I smile at her when she finishes, telling myself that sheep's head would have been worse. She smiles back and talks about the unique flavours for the rest of the night.

Before bed, we look at each other in the bathroom mirror while we brush our teeth. I adjust the collar of Nel's flannel pyjama top; a lifelong habit. We lie facing each other under the thick duvet.

'I do love you, you know,' says Nel.

'I know.'

She kisses me on the forehead and puts out the light.

***

Our flight home is early. I take a diazepam in the departure lounge and slowly feel my edges melting away. I stay with the bags while Nel goes to duty free to buy Brian a gift. She comes back smelling strongly of several perfume samples, notes of roses and something spicy. She feels stiff when she sits down. The anxiety is palpable. I offer her a diazepam but she refuses and instead ruffles through her duty free bag, pulling out a miniature bottle of wine. She starts to drink straight from the bottle and I feel my neck going red, trying to look around us in a way that isn't obvious.

Nel takes the window seat this time, and I sit between her and a young Icelandic man who tells me he is travelling to Edinburgh for an interview at the university. We have only been in the air for twenty minutes when the pilot makes an announcement. He tells us that from the left side of the aircraft, it is possible to see the northern lights. He switches off the fasten seatbelt sign. Those on the right side of the plane rush out of their seats, phones in hand, leaning over the knees of strangers to try and see the phenomenon. I worry the plane is about to tip.

A space opens up near the window by the emergency exit in front of us. I feel light from the medication, and get up. The sky is luminous, the green is electric, it's sea green and it's acid green and there's a purple snake darting through the middle. I watch the ethereal dance and it is so beautiful that I feel it like a dull ache in my chest. The wisps twist and curl and float like ghosts. I turn to look at Nel. She is still in her seat, eyes closed. The pilot says that the seatbelt sign will be turned on again very soon. I hurry over to her, shake her arm.

'You need to see this.'

She looks at me in a new way and says, 'I can't.'

'What? Don't be silly; just look over by the exit and you'll see it.'

'You don't understand,' she says.

Icelandic boy is watching us, legs twisted round into the aisle to let me through.

I wait for her to say something more. She takes a sip of wine and wipes her lips on the back of her hand.

'I can't do any of this,' she says.

Andrés Ordorica

IKEA

We are walking along aisles constructed as homes. Rooms to be exact. Model rooms of fake people that hope to inspire. Personas, I think is the industry term.

Edel — Edel is thirty-two, a graphic designer who loves to cycle and lives alone in a studio apartment. She likes loud colours and plastic dinnerware. She has a cat named Sebastian and copies of i-D magazine on her coffee table-cum-bed-cum-ironing board. Edel and I are not a match.

—You should buy a hamper. For laundry, she clarifies.

Moses sailed down the Nile in a hamper. A basket to be precise, but I don't tell her this. That would be a weird non-sequitur. She is an atheist, so my catechism facts would bear little interest. I nod and pick up a hamper named Frumpkït and put it in our trolley. I thank her for the suggestion. Mother-in-laws always have suggestions. Son-in-laws are always nodding.

We stop at Josiah. Josiah is a wealthy IT executive living in a pristine penthouse. He likes marble and steel. Josiah is not husband material, probably has had one too many STI scares but is handsome. At least he has pretty wine glasses to serve Merlot in for 'overnight guests' who quietly let themselves out afterwards.

Josiah does not fit the aesthetic I am going for, that we are going for. The truth is I hate flat-pack furniture, and the crowds and size of IKEA set my anxiety off. Everything feels and looks mass produced and rarely inspires. I long for something vintage, unique, something that has a story to it. A writer on the hunt for character, is what she says to me. We laugh at that.

My mother-in-law loves charity shops. We are now attempting to find a treasure. This is five months later during a family holiday in the south of France. Somewhere in a small town on the Mediterranean, we both happen upon a shop. The husbands are back at the hotel, reading newspapers and drinking espressos while fighting off red wine hangovers from the night before.

We conspire in the narrow paths of a cramped antique shop. An emerald cut decanter, square topper, treasure of all treasures stands before us.

—Your green kitchen, she says aloud.

— What green kitchen?

— The dream kitchen. You once told me that your dream kitchen is green. Wouldn't that be lovely on the counter?

It would be. Sitting on the counter as I cook, I would finger the sharp cuts of glass, calming myself as guests make small talk in the dining room. My emerald jewel, heirloom bought in France and passed down to my future great-great grandchildren.

Moira. That's her name. Scottish as can be, votes SNP, hand stitches Saltire flags and serves Tunnock's cakes with tea. She is that kind of Scot.

— Affa bonnie, I say to her.

Proud of my Doric. Look at me, brown boy speaking Doric in some antique shop in the south of France. It's what all this is: awfully beautiful.

We are now in a cramped living room in Aberdeen; a post-war council house. Somehow, we fit together like puzzle pieces, eight of us on two sofas this summer afternoon. Who drinks hot tea when it's 72 degrees Fahrenheit outside?

— A hot tea will cool you down, his grandma says to me while clutching pearls.

Fit fit fits fit fit? Come again, mouth a gap. They laugh. He grabs my hand slyly and mouths, 'I am glad you're here.' The first time meeting the whole family. Not as big as my Mexican family, but just the right size to all fit in a cramped living room like this.

His grandad interjects. It's Doric he explains. Which foot fits which foot? Shoes, the joke is about shoes. Must Google later if Doric is an official language of Scotland. If we marry, will I have to become fluent?

It's a week later. The sun is scorching. Scottish summers my arse! A piping band descends upon us. What's your tartan? My tartan, I quip. Do they have a tartan with tacos, Negro Modelo and Catholic guilt sewn into the cloth?

Me and him. We are in the Chieftain's tent sharing a dram of whisky. The whisky and I are the same colour. He looks at me and I know he is deeply in love with me and that scares me to death. I shot the dram.

—You're supposed to sip it, he reprimands.

Well, you're supposed to not fall in love with me. Hit me, I say in a loud American accent. In horror, the Chieftain politely pours another. I sip it this time and march out of the tent. The Highlands look purple today.

We are now on a canal, an autumn afternoon. He is visiting me, and we are walking together. He stops.

— I have a question.

Always questions, he knows how much I hate questions. I always have.

Back at IKEA, Moira points to a couch. You should look at that. It's very reasonably priced, don't you think? Questions, always questions.

If you asked me when I was sixteen, 'Do you think you'll marry?' I'd have said no. That is to say, back then gays didn't marry, and I was not yet gay. That is to say, I was not out and so I would probably have just responded to the question with a sheepish, 'Umm, not sure.'

— Are you listening?

— It's raining, I tell him.

And, it was, when he finally bent down with a vintage silver ring in his hand. A treasure from an antique market. Like mother, like son. He done good.

— Marry me?

In 2014, same-sex marriage became legal in Scotland. So many questions came out of this because of our new-found rights. What do you wear to a gay wedding? Do you both wear matching outfits? That would be a bit too much, too on the nose. I mean, we are gay, not twins. We have two distinct personalities. He is calm, I am haughty. He reads Gore Vidal, I read conspiracy theories about when Beyoncé is releasing her next album. Like his parents, he is a member of the SNP. I am a member of the Beyhive. Would this work? What is the precedent and who do you turn to for advice on gay marriage?

Marriage is marriage is marriage. Love is love is love. Mantras I sing to myself. My own mother, over lunch, says to me that this is a partnership, a friendship for life. What is her advice? If you want a marriage that works, then you need to always be open and always champion each other.

— Will you answer the question?

— Yes, yes, let's get married!

We finally load the car, purchases made. My in-laws drive me down cobbled streets to our new flat. Their son is away on business, my husband, but they are helping me run errands nonetheless. They unload the boxes and walk up our tenement stairs into our new home. They stop in the hallway and look at a framed photo from our wedding, they smile.

— We are so glad you are home (Scotland they really mean). Scotland is now my home.

My mother-in-law who is not one for convention gives the wedding speech. The room is full of our loved ones. I steady my eyes on a silver punch bowl that has carved thistles on its rim. I try to not cry by holding my gaze on the bowl. Scottish people do not cry, Mexicans cry all the time. I nod as she speaks, saying kind words about us.

— He is your story and you are his. Your stories were always meant to end up like this.

We toast. This is it, isn't it? We spend our whole lives trying to find unique treasures that have stories. Something that will catch our eye, and then one day he walks into a dimly lit pub and you look up and you say, 'Thanks for meeting me.'

That's our story. Nae bad, right?

Jay Whittaker

NOT THIS AGAIN

I assume we're invisible
two women at fifty, plodding
through the heat, back to our car.

In my younger days I'd scan
the horizon more warily,
clock sunburnt men
clutching pints
ranged along the harbour wall
their backs turned to boats
bobbing on the Solway.

Lezzies!

So many years
since anyone shouted abuse
it takes a while to register
late onset outrage
at a statement of fact.
Like we care
what they think.

MAUSOLEUM

In the Playfair Library
someone has forgotten
to switch on the heating
and baby, it's cold inside.

From every ornate alcove,
blank marble eyes watch askance
as we shivering children of Enlightenment
are lectured on Brexit and data protection.

Peering at plaques on plinths,
we don't recognise these guardians
of a former order, their supercilious chins,
patrician togas, Victorian whiskers.

Reaching into bags for scarves,
pulling coats over our tailored work-wear,
it's chill as a morgue
under this splendid barrelled ceiling.

We could use some Empyrean fire
now we've made it
into the cadaverous ribcage
of the establishment.

THE CONTRIBUTORS

Alice Tarbuck is an academic and writer living in Edinburgh. Her first pamphlet *Grid* is published with Sad Press. Recent work has appeared in *Cumulus, Erotoplasty, Jungtaft, Datableed, Adjacent Pineapple,* Monstrous Regiment's *The Bi-ble*, and 404 Ink's *Nasty Women*. **@atarbuck**

Andrés Ordorica is a graduate from The Royal Central School of Speech & Drama. As a writer, he aspires to create liminal worlds filled with characters who are from neither here nor there. His writing can be found in *Confluence Medway, The Colour of Madness* and *The Acentos Review*. He has performed his work for Literary Natives and The Courtauld Institute of Art. **@AndresNOrdorica / andresnordorica.wordpress.com**

April Hill is a poet and prose writer currently studying in Glasgow. Her work particularly orbits her relationships with sexuality, intimacy, and the tensions between the internal and external worlds. She is most frequently found wandering between coffee shops in increasingly mismatched outfits.

AR Crow is a poet, performer and trainee psychiatrist. They like to explore the spaces in between. **@IAmACr0w**

Bibi June is a non-binary performance poet and theatre maker based in Glasgow. They co-founded spoken word theatre company 'In The Works'. Their work focusses on race, queerness, mental health and social inequalities. Their first pamphlet *Begin Again* was published by Speculative Books in December 2017. **@BibiJuneS / InTheWorksTheatre.com**

BD Owens lives near Helensburgh. His poem 'Home Coming' was published in *New Writing Scotland: Talking About Lobsters, issue 34*, and 'An Ear Trumpet for the Earth' was shortlisted for the Jupiter Artland Inspired to Write: Poetry and Prose Competition. In 2017, he gained an MFA in Art, Society & Publics from DJCAD. **@B_D_Owens**

Callum Harper is an aspiring poet born and raised around the South Lanarkshire area. Between writing and submitting, he is currently working towards a bachelor's degree in English at Edinburgh Napier University. 'To Be Divine' is his first published poem. **@Callum_Harper_**

Christina Neuwirth is a writer and researcher based in Edinburgh. Her recent publications include the essay 'Hard dumplings for visitors' in 404 Ink's *Nasty Women* (2017), and her surreal novella *Amphibian* (Speculative Books, 2018), which was shortlisted for the Novella Award 2016.
@ChristinaNwrth / christinaneuwirth.com

Ciara Maguire is a writer and community organiser. She writes about LGBTQ culture and relationships and has written a number of short films with filmmaking collective Lock Up Your Daughters. She was named one of the Young Womens Movement '30 under 30 Inspirational Women' for her work with Free Pride.

Elaine Gallagher has published stories and poems in the *British Fantasy Society Journal*, *The Speculative Book* and *Thirty Years of Rain* anthologies. Her short film, *High Heels Aren't Compulsory*, directed by Annabel Cooper and starring Jo Clifford, won Best Scottish Short at SQIFF 2015 and was shortlisted for the Iris Prize 2016. Elaine is currently studying creative writing at Glasgow University.

Elva Hills is a writer living in Edinburgh. In 2017, she completed an MA in Creative Writing at Edinburgh Napier University, and was shortlisted by Penguin Random House UK for the WriteNow mentoring scheme. Her work has been published in *Shoreline of Infinity 12* and *Issue 4: Ink* of 404 Ink's literary magazine, and she is currently working on her first novel, a YA science fiction dystopia. **@ElvaHills**

Eris Young is a queer writer from Southern California. Their work explores themes of alienation and otherness, and has appeared in *Bewildering Stories, Esoterica, Scrutiny Journal* and *Expanded Horizons Magazine*, and the *#QueerQuarrels* anthology from Knight Errant Press. They edit fantasy stories at **aetherandichor.com. @young_e_h**

Etzali Hernández is a nonbinary queer Latinx fierce femme. They are a poet, coder, designer, photographer, DJ and No Borders organiser. They are the co-founder of Ubuntu Women's Shelter. They use poetry to express lived experiences and the politics entangled in it. They love pandas, emojis and giphys. **@topimorita**

Felicity Anderson-Nathan is a writer, tutor and freelancer. Her work has been published by *Gutter, Dear Damsels, Marbles Mag* and *FTP*, and performed at the Edinburgh Book Festival Story Shop and That's What She Said. **@flick_writes**

Freddie Alexander is a librarian at the National Library of Scotland. His work has been published by Knight Errant Press and *Gutter Magazine*. He has been a freelance journalist for *Scotsgay* and *Broadway Baby*. He lives with his boyfriend near the sea and hosts Edinburgh's Inky Fingers open mic night. **@FredRAlexander**

Garry Mac is a queer writer and illustrator, known for *Gonzo Cosmic, Tomorrow* and *Freak Out Squares*. He is currently working on a full-length comic *AION*, based on his Masters' dissertation on queer temporality in autobiographix, and follows that with a political queer comic series called *Praxis*.
@garrymacl / garrymacmakes.com

Gray Crosbie is a writer and performer based in Glasgow. They enjoy writing in the boundary between poetry and prose and have been published in journals such as *Litro, Popshot* and *Lighthouse*. In their free time they enjoy hanging out with their dog Rooney, drag shows and too many donuts.

Harry Josephine Giles is a writer and performer from Orkney, based in Edinburgh. Their latest publication is *The Games* from Out-Spoken Press, shortlisted for the 2016 Edwin Morgan Poetry Award, and they were the 2009 BBC Scotland slam champion. Harry founded Inky Fingers Spoken Word and co-directs the performance platform ANATOMY; their participatory theatre has toured festivals across Europe, including Forest Fringe (UK), NTI (Latvia) and CrisisArt (Italy); and their performance *What We Owe* was picked by the Guardian's best-of-the-Fringe 2013 roundup — in the 'But Is It Art?' category. **@harrygiles / wwharrygiles.org**

Heather Parry is an Edinburgh-based writer. Her work explores self-deception, transformation and identity. Her first novel is currently under consideration. **@heatherparryuk / heatherparry.co.uk**

Heather Valentine has been a proofreader, a receptionist, a student teacher, a tour guide and a call-centre fraud detector, and her interests include knitting, video games, nail art and weird films. Her stories have been previously published in *Temporal Discombobulations* and *Thirty Years of Rain*. **@heatheratops**

Jack Bigglestone is a new poet who feels like a child learning to ride a bike — proud, excited, hoping desperately he doesn't fall off. Originally from rural Shropshire, he now studies English Literature at the University of Glasgow. His current poetic interests include queer perspectives on the body, gender, childhood and family.

Jane Flett lives in Berlin, where she reads tarot, plays cello, and rollerskates down Tempelhof runway in hotpants. She's been published in over 70 literary journals, broadcast on BBC Radio 4 and translated into Polish, Croatian and Japanese. Jane is also one half of the riot-grrrl band Razor Cunts. **janeflett.com**

Jay G Ying's poetry has appeared in *The Adroit Journal, PBS Bulletin* and *Ambit*. He was the winner of the 2017 Poetry Book Society Student Poetry Prize and was shortlisted for the Desperate Literature Short Fiction Prize. He is a reader for The Adroit Journal and currently lives in Edinburgh. **@jaygying**

Jay Whittaker's debut poetry collection, *Wristwatch*, was published by Cinnamon Press in 2017. She writes about transition, resilience, grief, living with breast cancer, and LGBT+ lives (including her own). She performed at the StAnza international poetry festival 2018, and has recently appeared in *Gutter* and *The North*. **@jaywhittapoet / jaywhittaker.uk**

Jonathan Bay is a trans poet from California, currently living and working in Edinburgh. Currently pursuing a PhD in creative writing, he has been anthologized and published widely. In 2017, his debut pamphlet collection was published by House of Three.

Jo Clifford is a playwright, performer, proud father and grandmother. She is the author of around 90 plays. Right now she is performing her *Gospel According to Jesus Queern of Heaven* and her *Eve* (a National Theatre of Scotland production) in the UK and in Brazil, where her Gospel has been continuously touring for the last two years. Her five play sequence *Five Days Which Changed Everything* was recently broadcast on BBC Radio 4. Her first play *Losing Venice*, first performed 1985, is being revived by the Orange Tree Theatre in London; and her *Anna Karenina* has recently had a highly successful run in Tokyo.

Kirsty Logan is the author of the novels *The Gloaming* and *The Gracekeepers,* short story collections *A Portable Shelter* and *The Rental Heart & Other Fairytales*, flash fiction chapbook *The Psychology of Animals Swallowed Alive*, and short memoir *The Old Asylum in the Woods at the Edge of the Town Where I Grew Up. Things We Say in the Dark* is published by Harvill Secker in October 2019. Her books won the Lambda Literary Award, Polari Prize, Saboteur Award, Scott Prize and Gavin Wallace Fellowship. Her work has been translated into Japanese and Spanish, recorded for radio and podcasts, exhibited in galleries and distributed from a vintage Wurlitzer cigarette machine. She lives in Glasgow with her wife.
@kirstylogan / kirstylogan.com

Laura Waddell is a publisher and writer based in Glasgow. Her criticism, essays and fiction have featured in publications including *the Guardian, Times Literary Supplement, McSweeneys, 3:AM magazine*, and the books *Nasty Women, Know Your Place,* and *The Digital Critic.* She sits on the board of Scottish PEN and *Gutter Magazine.* **@lauraewaddell / lauraewaddell.com**

Lori England is a bisexual writer from Glasgow. She has a BA (Hons) in English Literature and Creative Writing at the Open University and juggles writing with bringing up her own tiny girl gang. Her work has previously been published in 404 Ink and by 3 of Cups Press. **loriengland.wordpress.com**

MJ Brocklebank has previously written for television, as well as writing the screenplay for the independent feature film, *Anna Unbound*. He has had two short plays produced and in 2016 progressed to the final stage of the Tron Theatre's Progressive Playwright Award. *Becoming Doctor Barry* is his first full-length play. **@mjbrocklebank**

Rachel Plummer is a poet living in Edinburgh. Her sci-fi pamphlet *The Parlour Guide to Exo-Politics* is published by House Press. She received a cultural commission from LGBT Youth Scotland to write a collection of children's poems based around LGBT retellings of traditional Scottish folkstories. She has two children, three guinea pigs and entirely too many books.
@smaychel / rachelplummer.co.uk

Ross Jamieson was born and raised in Edinburgh and studied English Literature and Creative Writing at the University of Edinburgh. He has previously been shortlisted for a New Writers Award from the Scottish Book Trust. If nothing else, he tries. **@rossmjamieson**

Sandra Alland is a Glasgow-based writer and artist. San has published three poetry collections and a chapbook of short fiction, and co-edited *Stairs and Whispers: D/deaf* and *Disabled Poets Write Back* (Nine Arches, 2017). Story commissions include British Council's Discover Project and Comma's *Protest!*, *Thought X* and *The Mirror in the Mirror*.
@san_alland / blissfultimes.ca

Shane Strachan lives and writes in the Northeast of Scotland. His most recent publication is *Nevertheless: Sparkian Tales in Bulawayo* (amaBooks); other work has appeared in *Gutter*, *New Writing Scotland*, *Stand*, *Northwords Now* and *The Interpreter's House*. He has also staged work with the National Theatre of Scotland and Paines Plough. He holds a PhD in Creative

Writing from the University of Aberdeen and was a Robert Louis Stevenson Fellow in 2018.
@Shane_Strachan / shanestrachan.com

Zoe Storrie is from a tiny village in Dumfries and Galloway but now lives in Glasgow. She graduated with a BA(Hons) in English and Creative Writing from the University of Strathclyde in 2014. She has since been involved in youth work, teaching and roaming the streets in search of cats. **@zstoz**

THE EDITORS

Ryan Vance is a writer and editor based in Glasgow. First published in *Out There: An Anthology of Scottish LGBT Writing*, he has since been published in *New Writing Scotland, Gutter Magazine, The Glasgow Review of Books, The Dark Mountain* and *F[r]iction*. He has also collaborated with Lock Up Your Daughters, a queer film group, on two award-winning entries into the 48hr Film Challenge. Between 2010 and 2016 he created and edited *The Queen's Head*, a speculative fiction magazine. He has also edited fiction for *The Island Review*, and currently edits reviews for *Gutter Magazine*. **@ryanjjvance / ryanvance.co.uk**

Michael Lee Richardson is a writer, producer and community organiser from Glasgow. Michael has produced work for Pride House Glasgow and LGBT History Month Scotland. Michael is a Scottish Book Trust New Writer's Award winner and a member of BBC Scotland's first Drama Writer's Group. Michael's first film *My Loneliness is Killing Me* — directed by Tim Courtney — debuted at EIFF in 2018 and won a BAFTA Scotland Award (Best Short Film).
@hrfmichael / hrfmichael.co.uk

A NOTE FROM THE EDITORS

Thank you to Creative Scotland for funding Queer Words Project Scotland, without which this anthology wouldn't have come to be.

Thank you to the writers who gave us their words, with open hearts and open minds.

Finally, thank you to the queers who came before us, who fought for our rights, who risked and lost their lives to allow us all to shout our shared story louder.

FURTHER READING

And Thus Will I Freely Sing: An Anthology of Lesbian and Gay Writing from Scotland (ed. Toni Davidson), Polygon 1989

Out There: An Anthology of Scottish LGBT Writing (ed. Zoe Strachan), Freight Books 2014

F, M or Other: Quarrels with the Gender Binary: Volume 1 (ed. Nathaniel Kunitsky), Knight Errant Press 2018

The Bi-ble: An Anthology of Essays and Personal Narratives about Bisexuality (ed. Lauren Nickodemus and Ellen Desmond), Monstrous Regiment 2018